Those Flat Share Girls
(Oh, How They laughed)

First published 2023

Copyright © Stuart Duncan 2023

The right of Stuart Duncan to be identified as the author of this work has been asserted in accordance with the Copyright, Designs & Patents Act 1988.

All rights reserved. No part of this book may be reproduced, stored in a retrieval system, or transmitted in any form or by any means, electronic, electrostatic, magnetic tape, mechanical, photocopying, recording or otherwise, without the written permission of the copyright holder.

Published under licence by Brown Dog Books and
The Self-Publishing Partnership Ltd, 10b Greenway Farm, Bath Rd,
Wick, nr. Bath BS30 5RL

www.selfpublishingpartnership.co.uk

ISBN printed book: 978-1-83952-593-3

Cover design by Andrew Prescott
Internal design by Andrew Easton

Printed and bound in the UK

This book is printed on FSC® certified paper

Those Flat Share Girls
(Oh, How They laughed)

Stuart Duncan

A collection of Light Verse reflecting
a 'Sixties' Youth and beyond

Including: Juliet Adieu

A Requiem for those Star-crossed lovers of Verona

To A Poet A Thousand Years Hence

O friend unseen, unborn, unknown,
Student of our sweet English tongue,
Read out my words at night, alone:
I was a poet, I was young.

Since I can never see your face,
And never shake you by the hand,
I send my soul through time and space
To greet you. You will understand.

James Elroy Flecker
1884–1915

Contents

James Elroy Flecker *To A Poet 1000 years hence*   4

1	Goodbye To School	9
2	One Warm Summer's Evening in Grovelands Park	19
3	My Generation	23
4	Swish. Swish!	29
5	Alex At The 'Fish'	34
6	Homeland	38
7	Girl In The Rain	47
8	Out With The 'In Crowd'	50
9	Georgie Fame At The Flamingo	
10	Those Flat Share Girls	114
11	At Last	118
12	Where Was I?	124
13	What Did You Do?	135
14	First To Go	138
15	Sermon On A Mount	142
16	By Starlight	153
17	Blayden Thane	155
18	Complete	160
19	They Moved Like Dancers	169
20	Completely Gone	177
21	As Autumn Falls	181
22	A Drink Before Christmas	185
23	Crushed Love	188
24	For Pam	189
25	The Joy Of Ballroom Dancing	191
26	The Daffodil Patch	196
27	Hold That Door	198
28	Woof Woof!	200
29	Juliet Adieu	243

Hello,

I don't know who you are but thank you for taking a moment to glance at this volume of 'light verse' chronicling my 'Sixties youth and beyond'. You might have groaned at the prospect of encountering another tedious saga of outrageous over-indulgence, involving much abuse of both mind-altering drugs and compliant 'dolly birds', but don't worry, my rhyming couplets contain very little of that nonsense.

The pieces begin with me leaving school in January Nineteen Sixty to commence my adult life in a decade that became known, (not surprisingly), as "The Sixties". On standing for the last time in the school's assembly hall, I reflect that, far more than in the classrooms, I had learned in this, slightly shabby hall,

The customs and the tribal rites
Of my society's birthrights.
The only half-taught shibboleth
That stays with us until
Our death.

And further contemplate that

I only knew that I'd be stirred
Forever by the telling word
Lifted up from Common Prayer.
A Vivaldi piece, a Bachian air.
'Emanuel', 'Jerusalem',
All here, within this hall, consumed;
And 'A Wop Bop A Loo Bop A Whop
Bam Boom!'

And so, I was set to go. To discover that

Never in all history
Had a generation been born so free

And by the final years of their life 'My Generation'

‐‐ *found*
They drew a bye through every round

So, without any outrageous, hedonistic excesses, you will find that the life chronicled was not plagued by hardship. Although, that doesn't mean there were no regrets along the way. For instance, I'd seen in the crowd and on the stage at various music venues some faces who were soon to become internationally famous. I'd even exchanged the odd pleasantry with some of them, like: 'Alexis is really "cooking" tonight, isn't he?' ('Hip talk'?) But when their early breakthrough came. 'Where Was I?'

Far from the fuss and ballyhoo
I was on my way to Kathmandu

And, like most people's early ambitions, the dreams of fortune and fame that I nurtured in my youth just seemed to evaporate as I lived my life. This sorry state of affairs is brought home to me when I accidentally revisit the small, village of Blayden Thane, the sort of rustic idyll in which Constable might have found a hay wain nestling by a pond. I had encountered this village not long after I had left school and, strolling its lanes, breathing hawthorn perfume from the hedgerows, made such grand plans for my future life. But, returning again in my middle years, I find:

*Nothing remained
Of Blayden Thane
Just a concrete wall
Of urban sprawl*

And ponder

*Where had flown my only youth?
Could I not claim it again?
Sat there alone
I was shown
The truth:
It was gone like the lanes
That were once Blayden Thane's*

Ah, well. That's life I guess! But we carry on.

And, late in my life when reluctantly minding an old friend's dog in whose company I've enjoyed 'walkies' in the park, I sit and gaze contentedly at the disparate crowd surrounding me and contemplate:

*There really is no better place
To see first hand the changing face
Of our ancient, noble 'Island Race'
Than the local park on a Sunday morn
Where one can witness the brave, new dawn
Of a Nation being reborn.*

I hope you will read some more and, of course, be encouraged to buy a volume to read by the fireside.

Stuart Duncan

I didn't leave school at the end of the summer term with the rest of the crowd, so I was not part of the de-mob rampage that marks the last day of most pupils' school life. I had signed on for an additional sixth-form term in order to re-take my O levels, (not expecting to pass many at first sitting). But some serious last minute revision scraped me through all of my subjects at first attempt. I therefore found myself at something of a loose end, mooching around in half-empty classrooms with nothing much to do. I had loved my school days but I finally did what most people do: I got a job; and slipped away quietly on my own two weeks after the Christmas break. It was January 1960.

Goodbye To School

How different might my life have been
Had I learned to play the violin?

Darkened now and very still
The corridors I knew so well
Were leading me, quite volunt'rily,
On what I knew was going to be
A sorry stroll but memorable:
My last, self-guided tour
Of school.

For years this labyrinth had been
The backdrop to my life's routine.
But now, behind doors loosely closed,
The empty classrooms in repose
Gave not one sign that I could tell
Of wishing me a fond
Farewell.

Had they ever been aware
That, for a while, I'd loitered there?
Was I about to leave this place
With no residual mark or trace
To be in some long-lasting way
A small memento of
My stay?

     *

This modest local grammar school,
Like others of its kind,
Was modelled on the disciplines
You might expect to find
In those grander institutions where
The gentry's offspring were prepared
To step onto the nation's stage
And shape the future of their age:
The Church and guild and public schools
Behind whose secret, cloistered walls
The progeny that privilege sired
Were taught, in essence, to
Aspire.

Well I had aspirations, too!
Don't laugh! It's not a joke.
But hindsight's all too perfect view
Unmasked them as mere smoke:
To build a city by the sea
And name it, humbly, after me.
If this were true then you'd expect
I'd've studied as an architect.
But the still and silent classrooms knew,

The corridors had witnessed, too,
That all I'd ever done in school
Was mess around and play
The fool.

'Who cares?' I felt inclined to shout,
Lips curled in a sneer.
Like Eddie Cochran being caught out.
But the truth is: I did care.
And salt stings pricked behind my eyes
To look around and realise
That the chance of being classic'lly taught,
A prize for which my forbears fought,
Instead of being a cherished gift
Had simply been allowed to sift
Through the fingers of each hand
Like so much dry and drift-
-ing sand.

*

Pressing onward with my tour
I ventured up the final stairs
To where a lofty passageway
Was proudly boasting a display
Of musty, gilt-framed photographs
All chronicling the school's
Rich past.

Illustrious alumni
Who'd fared much better there than I
Were hung above me, looking down,
Each one in an Oxbridge gown.
And pride was glinting in their eyes
To clutch their hard won glittering prize.

I gazed up regretfully
To know this immortality
Had, somehow, not been granted me.
With valid reasons, I agree.
But was I doomed to always be
An unremarked nonent-
-ity?

And not just the classroom swots
Were pictured in these hallowed slots.
The school had, fairly, given space
To pupils who deserved a place:
Ill-lit in the semi dark
Were others who had left
Their mark:

Sportsmen with their heads held up
Each clutching at a polished cup.
And, set out neatly in long rows
Were cast shots of the old school shows.
Where, frozen in the camera's flash,
Was a fine, wide range of pup-
-ils past.

Most of all I loved these shots
Showing as they did, a cross-
-Selection of the humbler ones,
The common herd of also-rans,
Who'd stepped up keenly for a laugh
Encouraged by indul-
-gent staff.

Although centre stage, it's true,
Was dominated by the few
Whose portraits could be seen elsewhere;
The crowded chorus at the rear
Contained a wonderful array
Of humdrum children of
The day.

Freckled fat boys, tearaways,
Pretty girls, their eyes ablaze.
Amused and not the least perturbed
That all their costumes looked absurd.
Clearly they'd enjoyed the fun
Of 'doing' a Gilbert and Sull-
-ivan.

Progressive critics might declare
That "Youth" demanded different fare.
But "Youth" within my own small crowd
Always clapped and laughed out loud
When the Captain of the Queen's Navee
Claimed to 'hardly ever' drink
At sea.

Whatever whims might come and go
Intelligence will always know
When it meets excellence full on.
We didn't need an Oxbridge don
To feed us academia's twat.
Our school had shown us what
Was what.

Putting these moot points aside
I slowly eased my onward stride.
Because I knew, ahead of me,
Waited a schoolboy fantasy:
A young girl on the cusp of prime,
From thirty years before
My time.

Appearing first at, say, fourteen
Her slender body hardly seen,
But such a smile adorned her face
To me, it gave her pride of place.
And by next year, fished from the pool,
She was a radiant Maid
From School.

Then, at last, at centre stage
A poised young lady, come of age.
Mature and graceful in her stance;
A soft, warm passion in her glance.
Like a sleek and half-tamed panther
She was the Faerie Queen Io-
-lanthe.

Just how foolish can it be
To fall in love so hopelessly
With some old photos in their frames;
But I stood there just the same.
I almost whispered loud her name;
But that would mean I'd gone
Insane.

Knowing there was more to come,
I took a breath and sauntered on
To a portrait, further down
Of her in her Oxbridge gown.
With a smile that seemed to say: 'Tee hee.'
A burnished fiddle on
Her knee.

This was finally goodbye.
I gazed at her and gave a sigh.
Then pondered on a thought once more
That had often crossed my mind before:
'How different might my life have been
Had I learned to play the vi-
-olin?'

*

Some swing doors now confronted me
That led to downward stairs.
This would be the final phase
Of my self-guided tour.
The stairs, I knew, would turn and fall
Into the school's assembly hall
And, as I pushed the doors apart,
My body gave a sudden start.
The sixth-form choir was in full voice
And 'Kerry Dancers' was their choice.
Quite eerily, it seemed to be
That their performance was
For me.

This large and slightly shabby hall,
Complete with its huge stage,
Performed a multitude of roles
Throughout the long school days.
In the morning it heard Songs of Praise
Often with all voices raised.

Then it was our gym, of course,
With rubber mats and pummelled horse.
But Friday lunchtime it transformed
To a dance floor for the upper forms.
And then we lost all self-control
In the fever that was Rock
And Roll.

This hall, to a great degree,
Had served in educating me.
The customs and the tribal rites
Of my society's birthrights
Had been instilled quite subtly
That, now, quite clearly I
Could see.

Standing unseen in the gloom
I studied the enormous room.
Imagining my Faerie Queen
And how her days here would have been.
She must have joined the orchestra
But would her voice have graced
The choir

Had her sweet voice entertained
The Kerry Dancers' lilting strain?
But I wondered, more especially,
If she had danced the same as we.
Had that body, lithe and slim,
Done the Charleston in
The gym?

Had she, in this very hall,
Been inducted and enthralled
By that grandiloquent poetry
That forms the bedrock of our creed.
The only half-taught shibboleth
That stays with us until
Our death.

I only knew that I'd be stirred
Forever by the telling word
Lifted up from Common Prayer.
A Vivaldi piece, a Bachian air.
'Emanuel', 'Jerusalem',
All here, within this hall, consumed;
And 'A Wop Bop A Loo Bop A Whop
Bam Boom!'

My education had begun.
It was down to me to make it run.
I knew I'd never use again
A logarithm or a sine
But the trappings of a cultured mind
I knew exactly where
To find.

The Kerry Dancers on the stage
Had reached their piper's final phase.
Still a shadow against the wall
I eased myself from this great hall.
And with a final, unheard sigh
I gave my school a nod:
Goodbye.

* * *

One Warm Summer's Evening In Grovelands Park

..... what might seem no more than a fey,
Shallow and vapid fashion display.

One warm summer's evening in Grovelands Park
Right at the Sixties very start,
We strolled round the lake, a mate and I,
Shooing the ducks and admiring the sky.

We were set on a saunter to join the crowd
In a coffee bar that was then in vogue.
A leisurely stroll that we'd often pursued
We didn't expect to feel anything new,

But as we trudged on at our ambling pace
We both felt the clutch of euphoria's embrace.
That glorious warm sun, hanging ripe as a peach,
Seemed, like life itself, within our reach.

We'd finished our school days and, m'raculously,
Secured the certificates to help us proceed.
Now we were set to choose a career
Although what that might be we had no idea.

At sixteen years old, we were in our prime.
Poised, as they say, at our 'moment in time'.
And never before in all history
Had a new generation been born so free.

We felt all around us a changing mood:
A totally different attitude.
To say 'revolution' would be too strong.
But a transformation was coming along.

To try to express what this ground shift might be
Would sound like a hollow apology
For what might seem no more than a fey,
Shallow and vapid fashion display.

Be that as it may, we felt more than pleased
To be warmed by the sun on that glorious eve.
We felt well prepared to join the parade
When the bass drum was beaten and trumpets were played.

That week we had been on a shopping spree
Checking store windows for what we could see.
Didn't have much cash to splash around
Still, we were pleased with what we had found.

Quite by chance we had followed our feet
To a Soho back alley called Carnaby Street.
Where discreet small boutiques had traditionally made
Garments designed for the 'chorus boy' trade.

But a new shop now boasted a window display
Of audacious designs less overtly 'outré'.
We'd feasted our eyes on the stock they'd begotten:
Cheesecloth and denim and striped Madras cotton.

He'd bought a great shirt in blue gingham check
I'd gone for green denim with a collarless neck.
This gear was perfect for warm summer days.
He'd even bought slip-ons of powder blue suede!

But, as we strolled on, one observable fact
Came to us both like a forcible smack:
We were the only ones dressed for the sun.
As if it were something that just wasn't done.

Much older blokes that we passed on the way
Were still in the suits they'd been wearing all day.
Badly cut worsted of grey or jet black
Salty white sweat stains circling the back.

Only one gesture had seemed to be made
To acknowledge the sun that had blessed us all day:
The jackets were off and over the arm
Shirt sleeves rolled up for extra charm.

And, oh, what god awful shirts they all were:
Five in a pack at Co-op Stores.
That yellowed, off-white terylene.
Utterly drab to the point of obscene.

As this sad parade went trundling by
We didn't know whether to laugh or cry.
I'm sure our objectives were chewing their phlegm
Saying: 'Cuppla poofters, look at them!'

But that was not our game at all.
It's just that we were quite appalled
To find neither pride nor vanity
Stirred in the shadowy shapes we could see.

Did they not dream or, well, aspire?
Was self-effacement their major desire?
Had they not once said: 'Yes, this is me!
But is this all that I want me to be?'

Perhaps the sea-change that we both foresaw
Would be style over content, nothing more.
But that glorious warm sun seemed to be on our side
We felt a new vigour take over our stride.

And it wasn't too long beyond this eve
That an army of like minds would start to perceive
A new optimism of attitude
That would tot'lly transform the nation's mood.

Yes, soon we would find that we weren't alone.
There was a fire about to burn
And of that flame we had both caught a spark.
That warm summer's evening in Grovelands Park.

* * *

My Generation

.... found
They drew a bye through every round!

Go back to the start of time
In any age or any clime
I promise you that you'll not find
A generation blessed as mine.

Born in forty-three or four
With the nation still at war.
A war of which we weren't aware
But victory would give us share

Of the hero's accolade
That stayed with us through each decade.
And when peace followed VE Day
A major change was underway:

We didn't fully realise yet
But a brand new social safety net
Would very soon be put in place.
And we'd be wrapped in its embrace.

A man called Bev'ridge had put thought
Into writing a report
That formed the basic draft template
Of what became the Welfare State.

The government was adamant
That this would be an end to want.
A simple, actuarial plan
To safeguard every citizen.

A small deduction from the wage
Of everyone of working age
Allowed the government to install
A range of benefits for all.

So, very swiftly, came a bill
That promised if you should fall ill
Doctors, nurses with their skill
Would give you treatment and still will.

Education, too, was free.
Basic three 'R's then, maybe
A chance for university
With new friends and a prized degree.

We weren't really old enough
To understand this sort of stuff,
And even in our later years
We took for granted these ideas.

What mattered most, at five years old
Was playtime, if the truth be told.
And what a paradise we found
To run amok and mess around.

Smoking bombsites everywhere,
A wonderland for kids to share.
We braved the ruins, quite unscared
And leaped from tank traps for a dare.

How tame and timid in its themes
Today's adventure playground seems.
With Health and Safety standing by
In case some little weed might cry.

Enchanted childhood, yes it's true!
And good fortune followed through.
National Service, that iron rule,
Ended just as we left school.

So we were never forced to bear
The sergeant majors and all their
Brutish, bullying jumped up airs
Of 'Shoulders straight,' and 'Cut that hair!'

And this omission did no harm
For we were never called to arms.
While other nations had Vietnam
We'd be at ease in Benidorm.

Then time came, we knew it would,
To seek an honest livelihood.
'Career objectives' sounded good
But concepts we misunderstood.

We weren't thick, we weren't slow.
There just were things we didn't know.
It truly didn't matter, though
That we weren't sure of where to go.

Jobs were there to pick and choose.
If things didn't work, we'd simply move.
We didn't have the time to lose
Hanging round for dead men's shoes

Trade Union action 'fore our birth
Meant that a man was paid his worth.
Thus had been forged a perfect pact
'Tween cash and proletariat.

We watched as, round the Western world,
The myth of collective ownership unfurled.
But capitalism was at full growth.
A nation reapeth what it soweth.

The joke has run a steady course
'Bout why a venture needs a boss:
Committees asked to create a horse
Give you a giraffe, or worse.

So, came the day to earn our bit.
We looked around for what might fit.
And if we thought the job was shit
We merely packed our bags and quit.

A reference once, for which I asked
As proof that I could do a task
Read simply: 'Could be first class
He just needs kicking up the arse!'

Do I really need to say
That a new job offer came next day.
Ohhh, what lucky, folk we were.
Not forced to grovel for HR!

No articles or signed contracts
Were fixed like shackles to our backs.
But personal pride would make us try
To do our best when we were paid.

A little studying at night
Helped us get the concepts right.
Then, knuckling down and list'ning well
Meant we soon picked up a skill.

So, when we felt like buying a home,
Which comes to most of us some time,
With some scrimping, cutting back,
We saved deposits for a 'shack'.

And here we come to, possibly,
The luckiest break in history.
Inflation and prosperity
Hit the price of property.

So those modest, little homes we bought
Without much effort or much thought
Have seen such increase through the years
They've made us paper millionaires.

Now we feel we've done our bit
And finally retired from it.
But not to simply sit and stare,
Sipping cold tea in a chair.

It's golfing breaks in Fuengirola
With others who are not much older.
Others, who themselves have found,
They drew a bye through every round.

I know that pensions've taken a knock
But is that really such a shock?
Very few have not reclaimed
At least as much as they put in.

And did their grandfolk ever draw
Enough to live on as before?
No they didn't and, what's more
They were mostly dead at sixty-four.

It's now a troubled world we see.
Who knows what turmoil might yet be.
But I'm so glad I had a class
In the generation about to pass.

* * *

Swish, Swish!

Shoo-pa-katow, shoo-pa-katow. Shishhhhh! P'swish, swish, swish ...

I bought my wire brushes in my final term at school
They were an absolutely essential prop in the art of being 'cool'.
I got them in Scarths in the Charing Cross Road
And carried them home in a Dobell's bag feeling so
Delighted to finally possess
What to me was, more or less,
The key to earthly happiness!

I already had the 'drum kit' in my room, beside the bed.
I couldn't afford a snare drum so I'd improvised instead:
A telephone directory and a saucepan lid. 'Nuff said!
I could hear the swish of those brushes deep inside my head.
Who needed Alvedis Zildijan?
When you've got an old tin can.
Now: 'Look out Shelley Manne!'

It was actually Gene Krupa who had initially become
My idol in the art of slapping brushes on a drum.
So, essentially, I'd also bought a pack of chewing gum.
But Connie Kaye, Mel Lewis, too, knew how to give it some!
To follow their footsteps was my wish.
To serve up rhythm in a dish:
Shoo-pa-katow, shoo-pa-katow. Shishhhhh! P'swish, swish, swish ...

But before I actually got into playing there was something I had to do:
Set up the bedroom mirror so I had a perfect view
Of me and my brushes in action, heading for the big time game.
I'm perfectly sure that Big Sid Catlet himself had done the same.
The great ones have their vanity.
We all pose, naturally.
Why should it be different for me?

I had the records ready: bits that matched my rhythmic style.
And I gave the phone book a flick or two while
Perching myself dramatically on the edge of the bedroom chair,
My heart pumped quite alarmingly to be so nearly there.
Then, from my small, bedside Dansette
Came the exquisite sound of the Brubeck quartet.
An ideal combination to kick off the first set.

The brushes on the phone book made a perfect noise: k'pow.
I was gonna learn from Joe Morello just exactly how
To drive a band from underneath and now ... !
Whoops I seem to have missed a bar somehow.
The quartet's in the middle eight.
Hang on, lads, just wait.
I'll pick it up. It's not too late.

And the rhythmic pulse seems to have changed.
Joe's flicking some licks that sound a bit strange.
Come on fellows. Stop messing about.
Give me a moment to sort this one out.
'Let's start from the top: a one and a two!'
But even the bedroom mirror knew
That I didn't really have much of a clue.

But I was not disheartened or in any way deterred.
I was just a beginner. Let's be absolutely fair!
I sorted out something more steadily four-four:
Mulligan's Walking Shoes. I'd give that piece what for.
And that baritone saxist knew
Just exactly what to do
When it came to setting tempos you could flick your bushes to.

I carried on with Line for Lyons then Barksdale gave a Bark.
I know it was early days but I felt I was getting a spark
Of something like inspiration. It was quite a sensation
To actually be in there as part of the band. Elation
Was lifting me off my chair.
The band was taking me right there.
Parents were knocking but I didn't care.

With a couple of hours hard swishing I was really getting the feel
Although Mulligan's shoes had walked so much they needed a quick re-heel.
And with experimentation I'd found
That yesterday's newspaper gave a better sound
Than the phone book so I spread
The *Evening Standard* on my bed
And slapped at the headline story instead.

With 'Cute' and 'Midgets' by the Basie band
I really felt I was up on the stand.
Slapping the paper and chewing my gum.
I was keeping good time and giving it some.
If only my mates could see me now.
They'd be amazed to see just how
Quickly I'd picked up the basics: K'pow!

*

In my final term's 'revision' class I soon began to find
The crowd of kids there with me had been left a bit behind.
Not just in their studies but the things that mattered more:
When it came to taste in music, they didn't know the score.
Still caught up in yesterday's
Rattling tin washboard craze
Of the long-gone skiffle phase.

Although a ginger-headed kid, known to be a prat,
Turned up one day with bongos, sporting an old straw hat.
But needless to say, by the end of the day.
A sixth-form teacher had taken them away.
But all next morning, if you went near,
From inside the staff room all you could hear
Was the 'Banana Boat Song' loud and clear.

*

But the crowd I hung around with beyond the school's front gate
Were really into music and could appreciate
My desire to sort of contribute
Some background rhythm while Al and Zoot
Blew their hearts out in duet.
Or the Modern Jazz Quartet
Sedately bonded set on set.

Most of this crowd had bought some brushes of their own
And used to practice daily in their bedrooms all alone.
Or sometimes, on an evening in,
We'd have some beer or p'raps some gin
And take turns on our host's wire brushes
While Anita or Ella sang like thrushes.
Giving the parents below hot flushes.

And it wasn't just a passing phase: a transient, silly schoolboy craze.
I swished my brushes regularly throughout my long lost youth's great days.
The time I wasted with this obsession.
I could have been studying for my profession.
And it vexes me to say
That, for all the hours I swished away,
I never really learned to play.

***

Alex at the 'Fish'

'OOYA! OOYA!' Everyone cheer.

Vamp: 'til ready to play
Vamp: the 'Chicago' way.
Keep the pitch low
But don't take it too slow.
Okay now boys,
Think we're ready to go.

It was just the best music around
A lovely, rich, warm, mellow sound.
They're up on the stand
So let's give 'em a hand:
The wonderful
Alex Welsh Dixieland Band.

Roy Crimmins on the trombone.
Al Gay's sumptuous tenor sax tone.
And Alex's cornet
Is gonna kick off the set.
Sip on your beer
And enjoy what you hear:
Jazz music simply good as it gets!

Tony Pitt's strumming: vrum, vrum.
Herr Lenny Hastings on drums.
And Fred Hunt's left hand
Really driving the band.
There was no better
Music in all the land.

*

Well, that's, at least, how we felt.
And I don't think we were wrong.
Of course there were other bands
Within the idiom
Who had a style, a sound, a touch
That we liked almost as much.

But we stayed loyal to Alex.
Although fame would pass him by.
Lots of bands became big names.
But Alex didn't try.
He would just smile, foot tapping, as
His band played the best Chicago jazz.

*

Back of the Fishmongers' Arms.
That's where the music went on.
Skip jiving pairs
Leaping up in the air.
I'm sorry for you
If you never were there.

Art Saunders there at the door
Chuck-er-ling into his beer.
Tweed jacket on
He was having great fun.
Watching the
Customers part with their coins.

And, keeping the trouble away:
A guy that we called 'Tasty Ray'.
If Ray came on hard
He might tear up your card.
And tell you straight:
'Sorry, son. You've just been barred!'

    *

Vamp: 'til ready to play.
Vamp: the 'Chicago' way.
Keep the pitch low
But don't take it too slow.
Okay now boys
Think we're ready to go.

Hang on, now. What's going on?
It's Herr Lennie Hastings on drums.
The moment is near.
It's almost here!
But just hold on tight.
Get it exactly right:
'OOYA! OOYA!' Everyone cheer.

    *

Alex died at just fifty-two years
Outliving, funnily, most of his peers.
The 'Edinburgh Gang' who ventured South.
Already well known by word of mouth.

Archie Semple went quite young.
Al Fairweather, too, and Sandy Brown.
None of them lived to make old bones.
But the music that they made lives on.

Every week of every year
Another 'alumni' band will appear.
Good guys with a right to claim
The Alex Welsh brand in their name.

Bye bye then, Alex, and thanks again.
For all of the good times that you gave us then.
But, for now, there's just one thing to say:
'Vamp 'til ready.' Then: "Take it away!'

***

---

1 *"Ooya. Ooyah! This was Lennie Hastings' triumphant exclamation as he successfully completed another drum solo. (Still heard in certain jazz venues to this very day from broken old men as they spill their beer in excitement.) Apparently, what Lennie was actually saying was: 'A-hoola! A-hoola!'*

Homeland

'Home Thoughts From Abroad' might be
'Is there honey still for tea?'
But ...

What does he know of his homeland who only his homeland knows?
Something along those lines the familiar saying goes.
Only the expatriate, dreaming in a foreign land,
Can truly appreciate or really understand
The constant yearning that swivels round his mind,
The aching and the longing for the place he's left behind.

The familiar sounds and flavours of a homeland you once knew
Will all your life remain an essential part of you.
Be it plantains lightly fried and coffee laced with rum
While from the local marketplace floats the sound of a steel drum.
Or chapatti and puy lentils with strong, black hot stewed char
While a Ravi Shankar student strums an old sitar.

Porridge richly flavoured with a tentative 'wee dram'
While from the hills a bagpipe serenades a rampant ram.
Liverwurst and Pilsner, frothing in the glass
Against a small, Bavarian band's insistent oompah-pahs.
Churros in sugar, sangria in a jarra
As from a dark bodega comes a tempestuous gittara.

These memories of your life will stay
Although your homeland's far away.
'Home Thoughts From Abroad' might be
'Is there honey still for tea?'

But when from time to time I've roamed
My prevailing dreams of home
Were hot buttered toast with bacon and a slurp of HP sauce
While Dickie Valentine's latest was playing on Housewives' Choice.

Yes, most people tend to find
A constant yearning for the place they've left behind.
But –

In far corners of the world I've met
A variety of people who'd set
Out from their homes to get
A possibly much better
Life elsewhere.

For different reasons they had said:
'I'm sick of home!' And chose instead
To reinvent the lives they'd led.
Or quite simply, they had fled from
Strife's despair.

I can understand the fear and stress
Of refugees who've been oppressed
By years of political duress.
But malcontents who've felt depressed
And told their fam'lies, more or less:
'Goodbye! Don't cry!'
Have always made me wonder why.

What event or circumstance
Has compelled them to leave with no backward glance?
How different were their homes to mine?
I think of my North London village the whole damned time!

*

My Village. My Manor. My Home

With eyes half closed and holding a ballpoint pen in hand
The poet whispered hoarsely: 'We'll call it "Metro-land".'

Perched right at the gateway to the Green Belt's leafy lanes,
Connected to the city by the 'red, electric trains',
My little patch of Eden was twinned with that terrain

Christened by a poet employed to add some charm
To the Metropolitan Railway's new-formed marketing arm.
Dreaming in his office of the rustic breeze; the calm.

The idyll of green paradise that He Himself might plan.
With eyes half closed and holding a ballpoint pen in hand
The poet whispered hoarsely: 'We'll call it "Metro-land".'

Well, facing north to Hertford we were slightly to the right
Of those swathes of unfenced pastures that were the Met's prime building site.
But in all essential aspects, we fitted the frame alright.

But don't confuse us ever with a dormitory town
'Dormitory' as in the sense of everyone's sleeping sound.
You'll find we were spoiled for action if you knew your way around!

And please forget those columnists who think their wit superb
When submitting copy for a Sunday paper's blurb.
They say: 'The "sub" is obvious but where on earth's the "urb"?'

Clever dicks and smarty pants with corks stuck up their arse.
Too obsessed with checking current thinking's weatherglass
To enjoy the simple pleasure of lying on parkland grass.

Speaking as a native I can only make this plain:
We had lakes and trees and tennis courts beyond our window pane
And Leicester Square and Soho just twenty minutes by train.

Yes, I loved my urban village.
It was a perfect home.
And it was only for a brief adventure
That I chose to go and roam.

I was glad to scuttle back there
When my wandering days were done.
There was a very real sense of returning
To the place that I belonged.

I understood the people.
Understood their secret dreams.
Their untold aspirations.
Suburbia's not the barren void that it sometimes seems.

Behind the privet hedges,
In white-net-curtained homes,
Fam'lies lived and bonded
In routines of their own.

Within a general framework
Of what might be called 'the norm',
People created lifestyles
Unique to them alone.

The 'children's education'
Was often at the heart
Of what became firm rituals
On certain families' part

This great consideration
And another point, of course,
The choice of entertainment
Was a major moving force.

For some it was a card game
For match sticks or hard cash.
Or a stroll around the local park
Giving pitch and putt a bash.

But I was aware of families
Who, more ambitiously,
Would delight in choral sing songs
With four part harmony.

Behind closed doors, with curtains drawn
People lived lives of their own.
While, beyond their iv'ry towers
Lay green parkland and fresh flowers.

Well, tell me just what
Is so wrong with that?

*

It is a known fact of life
That most are reconciled to
But residents don't know their homes
If they've moved there after childhood.

They know the street they live in, true;
And landmarks here and there.
But there are lanes and secret alleys
Of which they're quite unaware.

Beyond a certain age it's not
What most folk tend to do:
To run around in packs with friends
In search of something new.

But children from an early age
Learn to find their way around.
On pedal bikes or roller skates
Exploring their home ground.

They know the shortcuts through the streets.
Know each park and every square.
Know the apple trees to scrump;
And the places to take care.

Then, when they are old enough,
The normal course would be
To take a morning paper round
Which expands their territory.

And I myself, in summer months,
To earn a bit of wedge,
Would tour the district, shears in hand,
Saying: 'Can I cut your hedge?'

Apart from being a lucrative job
And not at all a chore.
It took me to some hidden streets
I'd never seen before.

Lanes and quiet cul-de-sacs
Where carefully tended flowers
Gave off a rich aroma
After sudden summer showers.

There's nothing like a garden
To invigorate the soul.
To create the earthy innocence
Of the village green maypole.

And my whole urban village
Became luxuriant in spring.
With a host of nurtured petals
Erect and shimmering.

So, by the end of childhood,
I knew my village well.
Knew the lanes and byways and knew the people, too.
Not just other children but older locals who

Served in family grocery shops
Or drove delivery vans.
They'd smile as I strolled home for lunch,
Or hoot and wave their hands.

And in my later years at school
I also got to know
Places that in days to come would see a lot of me:
Coffee bars and boozers where camaraderie

Came as warm and frothy as
The espresso that we drank.
Or beer that gushed in fountains from
Oak barrels or keg tanks.

Was it so unreasonable,
The strange delight I felt,
On walking into any bar or other rendezvous
To find it filled with friendly faces that I knew?

And was this casual fellowship
What really made me feel
That my suburban habitat
Was a 'native soil' ideal?

A happy home's not pretty parks
And council tennis courts;
It can be the most deprived of run-down, sink estates
If you get on with your neighbours and have a crowd of mates.

So was it that those folk I met,
Far away across the sea,
Were self-sufficient loners with
No need for company?

Oh well, that's for them to know
And live with as they will.
As for me, I loved my home
And dream about it still.

***

Girl In The Rain

Fifty years have passed since then.
I never did see you again.

You:
Girl in the rain,
Standing alone on a station.

Me:
Boy on a train,
Bound for no real destination.

Sat,
Wond'ring just who you were.

You:
Girl in the rain,
Looking around you so sadly.

Me:
Boy on a train,
Wanting to know you so badly.

Why
Did I just sit and stare?

Why
Didn't I stir from my limbo?

Stand
And wind down the window.

Say:
'Please, won't you journey with me?'

*

But the train whistle blew.
And I instantly knew
That I would never know you.

*

Then,
As the train left the station.

You,
Turned your glance in my direction

And
Gave such a wan, poignant smile.

*

Fifty years have passed since then.
I never did see you again.
The life I've lived's been rich and full.
Fate and chance have not been cruel.
And yet,
I will never forget!

*

So,
Girl in the rain,
How has your young life unfolded?

Safe,
In from the rain,
Did you find something to hold to?

Or,
Have you just drifted like me?
Thinking that you were free?

Yes,
Girl in the rain,
Never has one day passed by me

But
That smile that you gave
Has not been like a beacon to guide me.

Though,
I accept the fact now,
I never will know just who you were.

* * *

Out With The 'In Crowd'

The Approach

'This is what I'd like to propose:
That, tonight, I hang round with you
Watching exactly what you do.'

It was another Saturday lunchtime in the Mayfair coffee bar,
Most of the usual faces were there, as they always were.
Idle chatter as straws were bent.
Not much money being spent.
Mister Sawyer, whose place it was,
Was making a bit of a noise because
Too many empty glasses meant
He was going to be struggling to pay the rent.

Some of the crowd were making a fuss
Saying: 'Why are you always picking on us?'
Then a little man sat all alone
Listening to what was going on
Took out a wallet extravagantly
And said with a smile: *'This round's on me!'*
Odd behaviour, I think you'll agree,
But we accepted his offer happily.

And, as the others collected their freebies the man explained to me:
'I'm from the Sunday Echo. *Commissioned to come and see*
Just what a teenage 'In Crowd' might
Get up to on a Saturday night.'
Hearing him call us the 'In Crowd'
Made me cough and laugh out loud.
<<I'm in with the In Crowd>> I started to sing
And the *Echo* exclaimed: *'That's exactly the thing!'*

*'Our features editor's a man possessed
With a mission to keep the* Echo *abreast
Of current vogues and trends.
His pursuit of the ephemeral never ends.
It can be a bit wearing for an old hack like me.
But I need to earn a living, so I agree.'*

He was a small and slightly oily man, squinting through horn-rimmed specs
And he had a tiny tape recorder fastened round his neck.
Central Casting, more or less
For the role of Our Man from the Press.
He blinked a bit then leaned up close
Saying: '*So, this is what I'd like to propose:
That, tonight, I hang round with you
Watching exactly what you do.*'

I think my facial expression was saying quite a lot,
But, to reinforce my feelings, I uttered the one word: 'WHAT?'
Then I had to ask him why
He didn't stay home and watch paint dry.
<<We really don't get up to much:
No 'Dolce Vita' kind of stuff.>>
But he wasn't a man to be rebuffed
And the truth is I felt slightly chuffed.

That, from the noisy gathering there this hack had singled out
Our small group of playmates as the crowd to write about.
I gave him our favourite rendezvous:
A landmark everybody knew.
Said we'd be there about seven o'clock

He said: '*Hokey, cokey, old cock!*'
Then went to the counter to get a receipt
For the expenses he'd been forced to meet.

***

The Rendezvous

..... we have to be very careful that no 'chancers' tag along.
A hazard that the 'In Crowd' has to take as norm.

I'd told the *Echo* to meet us at what's more or less home ground:
A landmark of the 'village' and nationally renowned,
Charles Holden's traffic island: Southgate underground.

We were spread out on the benches, some puffing cheap cigars,
Waving at various village youth hooting from their cars.
<<It's good to be well known,>> I said. << It makes us feel like stars.>>

<<We're waiting here,>> I told him, <<'til, the stragglers have all shown.
But we have to be very careful that no 'chancers' tag along.
A hazard that the 'In Crowd' has to take as norm.>>

He didn't seem to note the irony in my tone,
As he scribbled in his notepad, getting it all down.
He really was an intense and earnest little man.

In fact the 'stragglers' weren't far off at all
Just across the road in Burton's snooker hall.
Doing their best to pocket that slippery black ball.

When at last they finally appeared
Everyone feigned a hearty cheer,
'Sorry, guys and gals, to keep you waiting here,'

Martin said, not sounding the least sincere.
'But some of the Runners were at the tables. 'Near,
I might tell you, to salty, bleeding tears!'

Since their promotion to Division One
The 'Runners' had been on a lucky run.
But with today's result it had come undone.

'Anyway,' said Martin. 'They're coping with the stress.
And Dipper's given me a likely address.
'Could be worth checking would be my guess.'

Saying this, Mart flicked into his hand
A cigarette pack of a full-strength brand
Then tapped the pack with two fingers and

Offered the contents around the crowd
While posh piece Luella exclaimed aloud:
'Oh, not in the street, Mart. "Nice girls" aren't allowed!'

'Well, put it behind that precious ear, you tart.
And save it for later on,' said Mart.
'I said we'd meet Varley and Vanessa in the Hart.'

'Then we might try Dipper's address. 'S not far.
Five minutes max in a slow-moving car.'
'Well, let's hope Skanky Skinner's not at the bar,'

Said Brad. 'Don't want him hoppin' in the back.
Making out he's one of our pack.'
<<See what I mean,>> I said to the hack:

<<'Chancers everywhere. It's a hazard of the game.
But I daresay old Skanky's going to get there just the same.
Now, we're heading 'cross the road. Are you still glad you came?>>

In fairness to the newsman, he got the first round in.
Although I said we'd get a kitty going. So, good for him!
But I noticed he got a till receipt from the barman, Jim.

Vazz and Vess were there already at a table of their own
They looked very cosy together and Vazz feigned a groan
As the crowd trooped over and Mart said: 'How's it goin'?'

He tapped his cigarette pack again and offered it around.
This time more takers took and he found
He was left with an empty packet in his hand.

'Should've put one behind your ear, dear,'
Luella murmured, leaning near
To the Zippo lighter that appeared.

And soon we were puffing clouds of smoke
Into the thick, grey fug, while sharing a joke.
We might wonder now why we didn't all choke?

'So, where've you sorted out for tonight, Mart?'
Asked Varley. 'We're not staying in the Hart.'
'Well, we might stay for a few 'fore we start.

But then Dipper's given us a likely address.
Just round the corner, more or less.
Could be worth trying is my guess.'

The *Echo*'s round was sunk happily
And Mart looked at Varley expectantly.
'Whose round is it?' he asked pointedly.

Varley got to his feet with a scowl
And rubbing a tenner across his brow
Said: 'It's always down to me, somehow.'

We sunk Vazz's round and would have had some more
But we saw Skanky Skinner slinking in the door
So we trooped out the back way before he turned and saw us.

We stopped in at the off licence to stock up on the booze:
Spent quite a bit but what had we to lose?
When we turn up at a front door we never get refused!

Then we clambered into cars with a concerted heave.
Girls on laps and windows down so that we could breathe.
The *Echo* got into my car and the convoy was set to leave.

*

23 Wilmington Avenue

But when +the door swung open we got a slight surprise:
A guy we actually knew was there before our eyes.

Twenty-three Wilmington Avenue
Was not that hard to find.
It was an imposing mansion behind walls, wisteria lined.
We knew as we stood at the grand front door that good taste lay behind.
But when the door swung open we got a slight surprise:
A guy we actually knew was there before our eyes.

His name was Simon but we couldn't shake hands
'Cos we were struggling to hold our 'party cans'.
<<We actually know this evening's host.>>,
I said to the hack at my back,
<<Or I should p'raps say, 'know him almost.'
We see him around quite regularly at every known outpost.>>

Simon seemed pleased to see us and opened the front door wide.
And we looked around us, awe-struck at what we found inside.
'Welcome to my cottage, guys,' he said with a hint of pride.
'Folks're away for the weekend and so
With free run of the place I thought I'd throw
A little bit of a party. They won't ever know!'

<<But, now we're in:
Let the party begin!>>

*

The Party Begins!

I feel a shiver down my spine
As I think that, if this place was mine,
I certainly wouldn't just go away
And leave young Simon holding sway.

Now, we're spread on the staircase.
We like to sit on the stairs,
It's the perfect place to check the door for guests as they appear:
The predictable perennials in small groups or a pair.
And we meet a constant flow of girls
Struggling loowards to brush their hair.

The ladies we had arrived with,
Old friends we've known for years,
Have all dispersed to look around to see who might be here.
Looking, perhaps, for true romance while we glug at our beer.
We're halfway through our first large can
Wishing all who pass us: 'Cheers!'

I whisper to the *Echo's* man
<<Yes, I don't want to shout
But we've got a suspicion that Simon would like to join our crowd.
Always waves if he sees us about.
So, if this party goes okay,
We might well sort that out.>>

Then I get a start to see
A familiar figure already here.
He must have jogged 'cos he never has a car:
It's Skanky Skinner, nursing a beer.
I turn to the newsman
And lean t'wards his ear.

<<Talking of hopeful wannabees,>> I say
<<See that poseur over there!
With the menthol cigarette and 'brilliantinoed' hair.
He hangs around us all the time and we have to take great care
That he doesn't sneak into a car
When the convoy moves somewhere.

Come on over and meet him,
Hear what he's saying now.
The things this bloke comes out with make us curl up on the floor.
His name is Skanky Skinner, and we all wonder how
He keeps up his performances
Without twitching an eyebrow.

Come on over and catch
P'raps jot down a snatch
Of his complete and utter twat.
You'll find he's one of those blokes
Who's very easily coaxed
To reveal his 'inner prat'!>>

<<How y'doin', Skanky?>>
I say with bonhomie.
And I'm greeted with a puff of menthol as he winks suggestively.
'How y'diddling, matey?' the poseur asks of me.
Then he's whispering in my neck:
'Blonde piece laughing. There! D'you see?

Begging for it. Gagging, mate. Trust me!'
He takes another menthol puff,
And sucks a quick breath before whispering confidingly.
'Yes, I think that later on I could well be doing my stuff!'
<<Made an approach yet, have you?>> I ask, deadpan.
'Not quite yet, matey. But soon enough.'

<<Are you taking this in?
There'll be much more to come.>>
And old Skanky doesn't let me down.   He's really on good form.
'Yes, to tell the truth, old chap, the sex life's pretty rum.
The Parisienne model I was seeing from work
Has been recalled to her home.

And, believe me, those Parisiennes
Really know how to fuck!'
<<I'm surprised the small insurance group you work for needs
Parisienne models on the staff,>> I cluck.
'Entertaining clients,' he whispers.
'They should have such luck.

There's just one tiny prob, though,'
He tells me, changing tone.
'I haven't got wheels this evening. Could I borrow yours?'
<<Borrow my fucking car?>> I shout. This was quite unknown.
<<The old man would take my keys straight back.
And how'm I s'posed to get home?>>

'I think she's with a friend, mate,
So p'raps…!' <<No 'p'raps' at all.>>
'And your dad needn't be concerned 'bout Skanky's driving skills.
I'm registered "advanced", mate and that's not even all:
I'm qualified for Formula One.
Just give Brands Hatch a call!'

I have to slap his shoulder.
While laughing at his front.
<<Oh please, Skanky, haul it in. You're going too far this time.
The only membership you've got is of the 'Berkshire Hunt'!>>
He twitches a smile and asks me:
'You calling me a cunt?'

Then, turning himself away from me
And rubbing his groin suggestively.
He murmurs out loud, emotionally:
'Yes. Begging for it. Just take it from me.
I might have to rent a room.
Let's wait and see!'

Then, addressing the hack
Who is scribbling in his notebook at my back:
<<So, what d'you think old Skanky's got?
Does the fellow dream or what?
I'd say his vivid imagination
Is fuelled by excessive masturbation.>>

*

<<So far the party isn't quite
What we expect on a Saturday night.
Plenty of guests around, that's true
But they're standing around with nothing to do.

The only noise you hear is chat.
Bluff and bullshit. Who needs that?
Trouble is, if I might say.
There aren't any records on hand to play.

This Simon doesn't seem to own
The sounds to drive the gramophone.
When we arrived things all seemed grand
With Duane Eddy's 'Guitar Man'

But seven times or more, since then
The King of Twang's been on again.
Should have brought our own Hot Sounds
To set the crowd's feet a-scuffling round.

Brad's got a case of forty-fives
That makes a party come alive.
But he left them on his bedroom chair
While he was distracted, combing his hair.

And Simon's parents seem to have
A state of the art new phonograph.
A handsome Pye Black Box, no less.
With overhead cam shafts and the rest

There are plenty of records, sure enough
All of it impressive stuff:
Deutsche Gramophone boxed sets
Of opera and string quartets.

Excellent music, I'm fully aware.
But it's not exactly party fare.
You won't find guests knocking over china
Bouncing around to Brahms B minor>>

And turning away from the newsman,
I find my gaze is drawn
To how the home has been adorned.
With fine examples of good taste
In evidence throughout the place.

A Regency standard lamp and shade.
A coffee table with mosaic inlay.
And, most impressively of all:
A Georges Braque painting on the wall.

I feel a shiver down my spine
As I think that, if this place was mine,
I certainly wouldn't just go away
And leave young Simon holding sway.

He's a likeable fellow, as I've said,
But just a bit of a weak airhead.
He doesn't seem to be manning the door,
Putting his hand up saying: 'No more!'

Thinking all this I become aware
That our man from the *Echo*'s gaze is elsewhere.
And, absently pulling at my sleeve,
He says: '*I can't believe*

That's Tommy Wilkins over there.
The 'Runner's' new captain, I declare.
And that's Frank Jackson for crying out loud.
Don't tell me soccer stars are part of your crowd?'

<<Not exactly 'part of our crowd',>> I confess.
<<But we see them out and about, more or less.
Most of the team live locally.
They share apartments round here, you see.

So, if word of a party gets around
They pop in for a drink 'fore heading to town.
Tommy's got style, I'm telling you.
Look at that mohair suit: powder blue.

And a Jaques Fath tie, loose at the neck.
But he can afford it with his pay cheque
Word is he's on thirty quid a week.
With bonuses on top. Makes me feel weak!

Tommy sometimes comes across 'a bit thick'
But he's a master of the overhead scissor kick
And he takes no nonsense from the lads on pitch.
One too many mistakes and you find you're ditched!

Come and have a word, if you like.
They might need cheering up tonight.
With today's result, they've got to be sick.
And I bet that Tommy's giving out stick.>>

Martin's already in there and chatting.
Not about football but playing at 'tom-catting'
One of the team has narrowed his eyes
To survey a young lady of considerable size.

'I'd say someone's been working on them,'
He murmurs with a sigh: 'Dirty, lucky bastard him!'
'Behave yourself, Dipper,' Tommy says with a snarl.
'I'm sure that she's a very nice girl.'

But Dipper's enthusiasm is hard to suppress
His eyes move to a girl in a tight fitting dress.
'Lately?' he asks her cheekily.
And Tommy turns round on him wearily.

'Keep it in your trousers, will you, Dip.
And try to keep a check on yer lip!'
But the conversation continues like this.
With the team blowing girls that they know a kiss.

Peppered with the vernacular of the day;
Expressions like 'aris' come into play.
And lots of things are deemed to be "ansome"
Or 'double smart'. 'I'd give that some!'

But suddenly the *Echo* stands back in surprise.
Hardly believing his squinting eyes
As Marigold Murphy bursts into the crowd,
Shaking his finger and saying out loud,

'Ooh, Tommy Wilkins, I'm ashamed of you.
Is that the best your lads can do?
"Defeat from the jaws of victory" it was.
You'll say it was just "unluck", I suppose!'

'Sorry, Mazz,' says Tommy, shaking his head.
'Weren't too clever, was we? Nuff said!'
Marigold is in full gear tonight.
Angora sweater and silk slacks, skin tight.

I pull the *Echo* away from the throng
To give him some background to what's going on.
<<The 'Runners' have no follower stauncher than
Marigold Murphy. He's their number one fan.

Guys who knew him from school all say
He was the best footballer there in his day
But he was never picked for the team because
Well, you can guess: just 'because, because …'

The story goes round that they tried to insist
He should go and see a psychiatrist.
The sportsmaster, an ex-army type,
Even suggested electric shocks might

Be the sort of treatment he needed.
Luckily this advice went unheeded.
Marigold was rumoured to say at the time:
'Stick the wire up his bum, not mine!

Like Popeye the sailor man
I yam what I bloody well yam!'>>
'Good for him,' the *Echo* whispers and I wonder: was it
Because he keeps a secret in his own little closet.

<<He couldn't have made the fixtures, anyway,
'Cos he went to dance lessons on Saturday.
And now he's a well-seasoned pro
Often in a West End show.>>

'*A dancer!*' comes the *Echo's* reply
As he scribbles some notes on his pad while I
Give him more background on Marigold:
A few further facts that I think ought to be told.

<<He's got three older brothers, quite differently made,
All doing well in the building trade.
And, in the past, if someone dare take the piss
They'd feel the force of a Murphy boy's fist.>>

The *Echo* dutifully scribbles this down
In an indecipherable kind of shorthand.
Then we turn back to the group, being discreet,
To find all eyes focused on Marigold's feet.

He is showing them a tricky move, but Dipper
Shakes his head and turns to his skipper
Saying: 'That twinkle toes stuff never wins
When you've got the opposition trying to break your shins.'

Marigold is out with his straight mate, Steve,
And Steve's delightful sister, both dancers would you believe.
They are an inseparable trio. All of them love to dance.
They look quite disappointed that they aren't going to get the chance.

The footballers, too, seem anxious to move on and, looking at his watch,
Tommy turns to his teammates and gulps down his scotch.
They'd done the early warm up. Now is time to go.
To make tracks for the Rheingold or the Whisky a Go Go.

The entire team is moving on with ladies at their side
And 'posh piece' Louella is in amongst their crowd
Talking to a girlfriend while distractedly
Pushing 'Dipper's' eager hand from where it shouldn't be.

My mate, Mart, is watching and comes up to me
Jerking his head towards the scene and confidentially
Whispers: '"Dipper" won't be dipping tonight,' quietly in my ear.
<<Not an unusual circumstance,>> I say. <<From what I hear!>>

But then I have to laugh as I glance back at the door
And look around for the *Echo* hack to tell him what I saw:
Amongst the chosen lovelies is Skanky's object of desire.
Clearly his oily ardour had failed to light her fire.

*

There must be sixty people here,
Smashing glasses, spilling beer.
And it isn't even half past nine.
Just wait until pub closing time.

'Oh, Simon,' is what I want to say.
'I hope that you don't rue the day.'
And even as I'm thinking it
A Tiffany lamp shade takes a hit.

It's cracked a bit where you can't see
And a girl's saying 'sorry' frantically.
But this occurrence will soon fade
Against the drama about to be played.

You've seen the Western Movies where
The town folk are dancing without a care
And the camera pans to the street outside
Where men in black hats have finished a ride.

Well, that scene, precisely, is set to occur
In what looks like being: the Wilmington Massacre.

*

Trouble Averted

... 'How utterly fearless must be a guy
Who has no qualms at being seen to cry?'

It is Simon himself who notices first
The presence in the driveway.
And catching a quick, involuntary breath.
He looks like a man confronted with death.

'Crimminy Crimpits!' he exclaims,
(He's not a boy for expletives.)
'The whole Biff Branagan gang is here!'
He looks around him in despair.

But someone comes up with a plan
And springs to his feet like Superman.
Roaring: 'Lights out. Heads down!
'Let's pretend there's no one home.'

As action plans go it is pretty lame
And Simon shivers and exclaims:
'Afraid we've left it far too late.
'Biff's already this side of the gate.'

It's me myself who has another plan
Feverishly I raise my hand:
<<Salvation Army>> I shout out.
<<Quickly, quickly. Sort it out!

We've finished the prayers, now it's hymns.
Have we got any tambourines?>>
I clap my hands and do my best
To start a sing song with the rest:

<<Let it shine on. Yes, let it shine on …>>
Gerry and some others know the song.
From Barnet Jazz club, years ago
When the Acker Bilk band stopped the show.

<<Let the light from the lighthouse shine on me!>>
Soon everyone's singing heartily.
I turn to the *Echo* frantically
Saying : <<It looks like the onus has fallen on me.
Sort me out a cup of tea!>>

Then, a shadow appears on the front door glass
And I feel my heartbeat in my arse.
But, as I step warily towards the door
I feel someone behind me taking over.

It's Marigold Murphy with a 'no nonsense' tread.
And I step aside happily as he moves ahead.

I realise that Biff's a scaffolder by trade
And relies on the Murphy brothers for some of his pay.
'Biff's a sweetheart deep down,'
Says the dancer, turning round.

'But he gets very emotional when he's pissed.
And lets his emotions go to his fists.
'What's the story: Salvation Army.
He'll think we're bleeding barmy.'

The front door opens and standing there
Is Biff Branagan: black leather jacket and yellow peroxide hair
Behind him twenty hooligans bouncing on their toes.
Their way of limbering up for action, I suppose.

But Biff's mouth opens wide as he sees who's there before him.
'Whatcha, Martin,' he says. 'Aincha got a show on?'
'Folded last week,' says the dancer with a sigh.
'Is there anything going in your line to see me by?'

(The dancer was also very useful on a building site
He particularly liked scaffolding work. You might
Well find him performing in all his glory
Leaping up the ladders as if he's in West Side Story.)

'Scratching around, mate, at the moment.
'Aint your bruvs got nuffink goin'?'
Then an ugly, little fat boy shouts from the crowd:
'Oo's this fuckin' poofter, Biff? Aint we goin' inside?'

Biff turns round immediately to confront the hooligan
With a look of rage and anger that would frighten Genghis Khan.
'You just keep your mouf shut, Percy!
You don't know shit from sugar!

You don't know your bolts from your bollocks!
Your arse from your elbow!
Yer dick from a dildo!
NOW THEN!'

He turns back to the dancer with a snarl.
'Sorry about that, Mazz,' he says like a pal.
But Marigold asks, 'Who's your fat friend, Biff,'
Giving a disdainful sniff.

And Percy, clenching both his fists,
Shouts: 'I aint putting up wiv this!'
'I aint 'avin' no fairy calling me fat!'
'Then you wanna lose some fuckin' weight, Perce. Simple as that!'

Biff's quick response brings laughter from his gang.
And one of them turns to the others saying:
'Biff's so quick with the repartee.
'Always got a comeback, 'asn't ee?'

And, behind the door, I'm laughing, too.
I'd known Biff Branagan from junior school.
He'd been in form Zed, though he seemed quite bright.
But I wonder how this will work out tonight.

The *Echo* brings me my cup of tea
And I decide to join in warily.
<<Hallo, Biff mate,>> I say affably
<<'Scuse me while I drink my tea.>>

Behind me the Wilmington Glee Club
Are trying to keep their performance up:
'He's got the whole world in his hands.
Whole world in his hands.'

'Fuckin' arseholes,' says Biff, turning to his boys.
'What for fuck's sake is that bleedin' noise?'
<<A mate's got parents in the Sally Army.
They're rehearsing for a show and asked would we
Come and make the numbers up as a favour.
Listen! I think you'll get the flavour.>>

Above the general discord of the untrained gospel choir
Comes the type of shrill soprano that is often quite admired.
But is an acquired taste which many folk dislike.
It seems to have Biff Branagan looking backwards for his bike.

'Fuck me gentle,' he says. 'Screw it!
No thanks, mate! We'll leave you bastards to it!'
And he turns round to his henchmen, still bouncing on their toes
It looks as if the scenario has reached a successful close.

I squeeze the dancer's shoulder, and watch the black, departing back.
<<You did really well, there Mazz,>> I say, smiling to the hack.
But, suddenly I realise that the singing has all stopped.
As if a choirmaster has given it the chop.

Will Branagan turn back now that there's silence all around.
Then, mercifully, there comes a new soprano's sound.

Not like the previous lady's voice.
Not piercing and not shrill.
A voice so soft and haunting that it sits on Wilmington Avenue
As a mist at evening will:

'Amazing Grace
How great Thou art
That saved a wretch like me.'

Something extraordinary happens as the voice continues.

Branagan stops dead in his tracks at the gate.
His entire black jacket seems to vibrate.
His powerful shoulders seem to be throbbing.
Then he turns round and I see that he's actually sobbing.

Biff Branagan, the brute, the bully, is crying like a baby.
Unashamedly.
'I'm a soppy, old sod,' he tells us quietly.
'But this song really does it for me.

Beautiful!'
He begins to join in softly.
His voice is not unlike the young Elvis Presley:
'I once was lost
But now am found.
Was blind but now I see!'

Biff stands there until the entire performance ends while, piously,
The gang are bouncing on their toes on the driveway, quietly.
They can plainly see
That tears are rolling down Biff's cheeks unchecked.
But they seem to be paying their leader respect.

'I'm a soppy old sod,' Biff whispers again.
'Don't mind me.'
Then he wipes both eyes with a leather sleeve.
And turns to face his band of thugs.
'Come on, you bastards. Come on, you mugs!'

And, moments later,
With a roar of accelerators.
The sinister presence is on its way.
Leaving me with nothing to say.

Except: <<How utterly fearless must be a guy
Who has no qualms at being seen to cry?>>

*

What A Party!

Everyone is dancing
It's a wonderful sight!

Safe back in the house again
Marigold is everyone's friend.
What could have been a nasty fight
Has, thanks to him, come out alright.

I thought that I had been quite plucky
But accepted that I'd also been lucky
To have had the dancer at my side.
That couldn't possibly be denied.

Skanky Skinner is the only guest
Who doesn't seem to be impressed.
'I'd just've told them all: "piss off!"'
He tells the others with a scoff.

'A bunch of yobboes don't scare me.
I've got a black belt in Judo, you see.'
<<That girl you were after,>> I ask.<< Where's she?>>
'Ohh,' he groans. 'Just another "Pee Tee"!'

There is still no music from the Pye Black Box
And so Marigold's trio shuffles off
To a late night Soho cabaret
Where they could dance the night away.

But good old Brad has been on the phone
To ask his kid brother, who's home all alone,
If he could pedal round on his bike
With the huge box of singles that we all like.

And now the kid's here, out of breath.
Clutching the box as if it meant death.
Brad gives him a shandy and a couple of quid.
Calls him a hero to do what he did.

Then, feveriShly, he delves in the box
Looking for something that really rocks.
It's a New Orleans classic that first comes to hand
Backed by Huey Piano Smith and his band:

'Ooh ee, baby, you've got nothing to lose.'
Frankie Ford's going on a 'Sea Cruise.'
Immediately the party comes alive.
Everyone is doing their own kind of jive.

It's been the perfect opening track:
We've 'got the boogie woogie like a knife in the back!'
But as the steamer siren fades away
Brad's found another classic to play.

A piano introduction gets things underway
Then Ray Charles asks us: 'What'd I say?'
Bedlam breaks out all around.
Everyone loves the Ray Charles sound.

Chairs take a tumble. Lamps go flying.
If she were here to witness, Simon's mother would be crying.
The guests now number a hundred or more
And every passing minute brings some more to the door.

By the time the single is flipped to side two
There's no room on the carpet for one more shoe.
But the elegant french windows at the room's farthest end
Are opened up forcibly which makes them slightly bend.

Then guests are on the patio, all down the trellised steps
That lead into the garden which is beautifully kept.

*

Everyone is dancing
It's a wonderful sight!
Everyone is dancing.
On a Saturday night.

Yes, they're dancing in the kitchen
In the hall and up and down the stairs.
They're knocking over tables
And they're knocking over stools and chairs.

Everyone is dancing.
And they're doing it right.
Everyone is dancing.
What a wonderful sight.

Go! Go! Go! Everybody.
Leap around and let it go.
Go! Go! Go! Everybody.
You're putting on a wonderful show!

Go! Go! Go! Skanky Skinner.
Dancing on your ownsome over there.
Go! Go! Go! Skanky Skinner.
Got less rhythm than your grandfather's wooden chair.

Go! Go! Go! Mister Bradley.
You really know the sounds to choose!
Go! Go! Go! Mister Bradley
You really know your Rhythm and Blues.

Well, jump up. Turn around.
Twist your hips and let them shake.
Bend down. Touch the ground.
How much rhythm can your body take?

Everyone is dancing
It's a wonderful sight!
Everyone is dancing.
On a Saturday night.

The party's really started now.
The front door's open wide.
New arrivals needn't knock
Before they come inside.

And they come and they come and they come.
Looking for an evening of fun!
Carrying cans in their hands
Or bottles of wine.
Nobody stands
For too long in the line.

*

I was very lucky as the dancing began:
A really lovely girl had been standing on her own.

So, we started to rock
And we started to roll
Laughing and cavorting
Like two demented souls.

But after a while she needed the loo
And so I said: 'I'll wait for you.'
But the heaving and the shoving of the dancing horde
Pushed me from the living room towards the glass front door.

And, as I'm standing there, I get a sort of shock.
A couple at the doorway have actually knocked!
They are clearly older than all the others there
And I think they both seem just a little bit scared.

'Is Simon here?' they call anxiously to me.
'Can we have a word?' they ask hopefully
'He'll know us,' they add in a tone slightly lower.
'We're Mary and Trev, the neighbours next door!'

'Oh dear,' I exclaim.
'D'you want to complain?
Is it the terrible din?'
'No. Not at all,' says Trev with a smile. 'We just want in!'

Everyone is dancing.
As the records spin round.
Everyone is dancing.
And they're loving the sound.

Yes, Brad is playing classics
And other numbers: totally new.
No one's gonna get arthritis
Sitting down at this Rhythm Revue!

Chubby Checker's done the limbo
And now another track's spinning round
Phil Upchurch and his combo
Insist that we don't sit down!

So get down on the dance floor
And grab yourself a bit of fun.
'Cos the next track on
Has just gotta be Da Doo Ron Ron!

Yes, get down on the dance floor
Grab any partner that you choose.
And get a piece of action
'Fore that black box blows its fuse.

Everyone is dancing.
What a wonderful sight!
Two hundred people dancing
On a Saturday night.

*

It must now be thirty minutes or more
Since my dancing partner disappeared.
I have obviously missed her
As she struggled back downstairs.

So I fight my way back through the living room door
Craning my neck for a sight of her.

An interloper seems to have taken over the sounds
And has chosen to switch the music around.
With an insipid and schmaltzy sort of pop
Aimed at young girls who like teenybop.

'I like it. I like it!' comes a nasal drone.
Followed by other songs of similar tone.
It is bland and insipid and so uninspired.
The best of the dancers begin to look tired.

I see the *Echo* has accosted a likely looking guest
Who's pulling faces at the music's change. Unimpressed.
Shoola prides himself on being 'a fool for rhythm'.
He's got his usual selection of 'collector's vinyl' with him.

'These new kid's groups have got nothing to say!'
He's complaining in a querulous way.
'The stupid songs and the chords they play
Have killed the excitement of yesterday.'

He takes an album from his bag and holds it in his hand:
Johnny Griffin and the Big Soul Band.
<<Wade in the Water!>> I enthuse.
<<That guy's really paid his dues.>>

'I tell you what!' The 'hipster' says emotionally.
(Using his sincerest term of flattery.)
'I tell you what!' He repeats to endorse his praise.
(It really is his favourite phrase.)

'This is the sort of sound DeeJays should be playing.
'Stead of this turgid crap! Know what I'm saying?
The UK's got bands that do this sound
But, brother, has the music bizz let a guy down!

The Yanks, if they ever hear this noise,
Will be laughing up their sleeves.
They'll shake their heads and hold their ears
Finding it hard to believe

That, here in the UK, we're getting this shit
While, over there, small studios make hit after hit
With music that's really got some Soul.
A genuine successor to Rock and Roll.'

He sounds very angry; even clenches his fist.
And at the next trite offering he says: 'Listen to this!
She loves you. Yeah! Yeah! Yeah!
She loves you. Yeah! Yeah! Yeah!

They're not musicians.
And they don't even care!
They just point their smiles at a camera
And shake their cursed hair.

In six weeks' time they'll be forgotten.
Replaced by other crap, equally rotten.
I don't even think they do their own playing.
Absolute wankers. Know what I'm saying?

No sense of adventure! No experimental drive.
Nothing that might keep the spirit of music alive!
You're into real music. Tell me you agree.'
I shrug my shoulders and say: <<Let's wait and see.>>

The truth is, I'm distracted
Looking all around
For my erstwhile dancing partner.
She just can't be found.

In the crush and the press
Of the two hundred guests
Who are packed into every space.
The lady I'm most interested in has vanished without trace

But the *Echo* interrupts to say:
'There's a conga underway.'
And, sensing he wants to get away,
I quip: <<Let's join in without delay!>>

'Aye, aye conga! Aye, aye conga!'
The line in the garden's getting longer.
Each guest desperately clutching the body in front
Kicking on the off-beat like a striker's toe punt.

A trellis of flowers has been brought to the ground.
Roses and delphiniums scattered around.
At the head of the line-up is Simon, I see.
Not really guarding his folks' property.

'Oh, Simon! Simon!' I think.
'Things are really getting close to the brink.'

After I've had five minutes or more
The conga becomes a bit of a bore.
So I ease myself out of the line and then veer
T'wards the kitchen to get some more beer.

But as I'm still fighting my way through the door
A young lady nearly pulls me onto the floor.
She's quite a well-formed and attractive young miss.
And she gives me a really succulent kiss.

But it's not the sort of guy I am
To take advantage or to do harm
To a woman who is keen to be kissed
When she's totally, utterly, outrageously pissed.

I vaguely know her and I know her friends
So I hold her firmly by one of her hands
And wave to a girl drinking lemonade
Then say, when she struggles across to my aid:

<<Get plenty of tap water in her.
And keep her away from Skanky Skinner!>>

Safe in the care of a friend she came with
She asks: 'Can you give uth jutht one more kith?'
I peck at her cheek and slap her behind.
Then head on to see what beer I can find.

But, more than fresh beer, uppermost on my mind
Is that lovely young lady who'd left me behind.

There'd been so much extraneous noise as we danced
That we hadn't exactly been given the chance
To get to know each other or
Decide whether I'd like to see her some more.

The numbers now are starting to thin.
It looks like the party's beginning to end.
There's only one final delight
To round off another Saturday night.

It's the almost compulsory 'Jellied Eel'
Where a bunch of the lads get together and 'peel'.
I turn to the *Echo* standing nearby, saying:
<<Have you got a camera to take a quick shot?
Or perhaps, after all, it might be best not.
Sometimes they get a bit cheeky and 'moon'.
While the crowd shout: 'Get 'em on! Get 'em on!'

Brad's got the single ready to spin.
So wait for the stars of tonight to come in.>>

And at the intro of David Rose's 'The Stripper'
We all know it's going to be a ripper.
It's not four lads who appear to a cheer.
But Vazz and Vezz dressed in each other's gear.

Her party frock on him doesn't fit.
So he's exposing her bra and one scrawny 'tit'.
'Off! Off! Off!' comes a chorus of calls
And 'On! On! On!' is the immediate recourse.

I see Skanky Skinner drooling by the door.
I don't think he's seen ladies' lingerie before.
And when the couple reach their bottom layer
To reveal each other's underwear.
So loose on Vezz are Vazz's Y fronts' bands
That she has to clutch at them with both hands.

Varley himself isn't quite so shy.
In her silky French knickers the guy
Bends over and gives us a shake.
So much excitement is hard to take.

But this really signals the party's end.
It's past two o'clock and folk start to wend
Their weary ways towards the door.

*

Across a Crowded Room

No golden, yellow moonlight holds her in caress.
No evening breeze wafts softly against the folds of her silk dress.

And, suddenly, in the crowd I catch a sight
Of the lady I'd been searching for all night.
And she is more achingly beautiful, more exquisite, more divine
Than I had fully realised. I want to make her mine!

Yes, there are girls aplenty
On show around the room.
Attractive girls. Sophisticated.
Elegant. Well groomed.
Many of them I've known for years.
They're charming and they're fun.
But they are Christmas candles
Against her August sun.

No golden, yellow moonlight holds her in caress.
No evening breeze wafts softly against the folds of her silk dress.
She needs no balmy moonlight. No tender evening breeze.
Her radiance transcends the mere effect of these
Set piece illusions. She is here and she is real.
No simple tricks of nature could enhance the way I feel.

In fact, she's got a scrubbing brush in her hand and I know she's noticed me.
But she's studying the carpet, pretending not to see.
Oh, the games we mortals play with our foolish, human pride.
It seems that she is hurt 'cos she thinks I left her side.

I edge myself towards her as she kneels down on the floor.
<<Oh, I'm so glad I've found you. I've been looking everywhere!>>
'Have you?' she says coldly. 'You seemed to be doing alright
The last time I caught sight of you, earlier in the night.'

<<Not that over-amorous girl who'd had too much to drink?'
I groan. <<Yes, I 'hit on her'—Is that really what you think?>>

Her brittle manner changes. She gives a little smile.
'I must admit,' she says. 'I didn't think she was quite your style.'
I laugh and touch her shoulder, say: <<Well that's good to hear.
How are you getting home tonight. Are you far from here?>>

'I'm with my sister, Mo,' she says. 'We only live next door.'
 She carries on with her scrubbing, hoping I'll say more.
<<So, I take it, then, that you've met Simon a couple of times before.>>
She laughs at this and tells me: 'I've known him since I was four.'

As she scrubs, her free hand just brushes against my side.
I have fallen in love with this beautiful girl. Her smile and her ladylike pride.
<<Is there any chance,>> I ask quietly.<<That I might see you again, maybe?>>
'You're very forward, aren't you?' she chides me, teasingly.

My heart is beating frantically. Like in a twee pop song.
She finds a scrap of paper and writes two numbers down.
'There,' she says, in a businesslike way as she hands the paper to me.
'That's me at work and me at home.' I take them ecstatically.

<<I'll be in touch, then. Soon!>> I say. Then: <<Look at the state of this place!
What'll Simon's parents say? It's an absolute disgrace!>>
'Yes,' she agrees. 'He let in riff raff from the street.'
And the smile she gives as she glances at me is more than simply sweet.
'But you haven't seen the worst of it,' she tells me earnestly.
'The things some people do for fun just really sickens me.
See those lovely records there!' She points at the filed boxed sets.
'The sleeves have been stuffed with smoked salmon slices. I haven't told Simon yet.

And that painting on the wall. It's his dad's prize possession.
It's smothered in tomato ketchup now. Needs cleaning by a professional.'
I groan in real pain as she tells me this and think to myself in alarm:
<<Biff Branagan and his Merrie Men wouldn't have caused half the harm
As the crowd of so-called 'middle class' kids who've been acting like philistines.
Rampaging and rioting. Were they out of their tiny minds?>>

I notice as I look around that Trev and Mary, too
Are helping to clean up the mess. That's what neighbours do.
I'm reluctant to leave this new love that I've found.
I really should join her with a swab on the ground.

But, lamely, I say: <<Well, I'll give you a buzz.>> And I'm warmed that, at this,
She stands up and gives me a lovely, wet kiss.
I slap my cheeks and shake my head, feigning a dizzy spell.
But, joking aside, something special's occurred and I think she can tell.

And then the *Echo* appears at my side clutching his precious pad.
<<Oh, there you are. Well, I guess it's just about time for bed.
Hope that you've made lots of notes
And picked up several useful quotes.
But now it's late and we've got to head.>>

So we make for the door but, on the way,
I just have to see her once more and say,
('Cos she knows that I love her),
<<Goodnight you old scrubber!>>

And then I have to rush
As she hits me with her brush.

*

I've given our man from the *Echo* a lift in my father's car
And now we're at Southgate station and I say: <<Well, here we are.
The last train left at midnight! So you're more than three hours late.
But, the taxi rank is open if you don't mind having to wait.

I look forward to reading the tome you're going to write.
About the fun to be found
On the outskirts of town.
But just try and get the facts right!

Oh, look over there: Skanky Skinner!
Someone has dropped him off here.
The absolute opposite of winner.
Looks like he's had too much beer.

His evening doesn't seem to have gone that well.
Just looking at him it's not hard to tell:
Now he's heading home half pissed.
For one more hand shank off the wrist!

It turned out a 'marvellous party'.
Hope you didn't find it a bore!
What's that you say?
'The hours flew away.
And you couldn't have liked it more!'>>

*

Homeward

.... this enchanted evening might
Not end as Just Another Saturday Night.

Beneath the orange street lamp's glow
How silent are the streets I know.
As, driving home with extra care,
(Because I'm totally aware
Of how much pale ale I've consumed,)
I long to be back home in my room.
And I know the first thing that I'll do,
When I've taken off each shoe,
Is spread the paper scrap I have
And dream that it might lead to love.
So this enchanted evening might
Not end as Just Another Saturday Night.

* * *

Postscript

I get a phone call during the week
From the *Echo* saying: '*Are you free to speak?*'
I say: <<Go ahead. Give me the news>>
And he tells me his piece has been refused.

'*Yes, the editor spiked it.*
Seems he just didn't like it!
Said: not at all what our readers expect.
No one sniffing cocaine. No outrageous sex!"

I'm on another assignment next week.
Doing the groundwork now, as we speak.
A place in the country, down by the Thames,
Where all sorts of Big Wigs spend wicked weekends.

Things go on there beyond your wildest dreams.
All sorts of shenanigans, or so it seems.
The sort of highjinks that make our readers drool.
Naked party girls cavorting in the pool

While major politicians mix with Russian spies.
When I saw the brief I just couldn't believe my eyes.
The editor's determined to get the story 'fore it breaks.
Maybe run it as a serial: it's got everything it takes!

'Well, if you need an assistant, young and able,
I could make myself available!'

***

Georgie Fame at the Flamingo

Georgie
Clive Powell was not Presley.
His hips did not gyrate.

Clive Powell entered the music scene
Through a stable door.
A door that several other young men
Had been ushered through before.
They'd been groomed by an impresario
Called Laurence (Larry) Parnes
Who had a reputation for coming up with names
Like Eager, Wilde and Fury, Fortune, Power and Pride
To create a vigorous image of Youth for the world outside.

Parnes insisted all his boys slap
Pig grease in their hair.
Made them scowl and mumble saying:
'Kid, you're really going somewhere!'
When Parnes first met Clive Powell he
Was just fifteen years old.
He played some nice piano and the businessman was sold.
But just as a backing band member drawing a minimum wage.
He was not to be the teenage idol taking over, centre stage.

Clive Powell was not Presley.
His hips did not gyrate.
But still, it's strange that Mister Parnes completely failed to spot
That this kid had a scorching voice
Which his other 'stars' did not!

But, just the same,
He changed his name,
As was his usual form.
He thought a while
Then gave a smile
And 'Georgie Fame' was born!

*

The Flamingo

The band on the stand then began the Big Blow.
They biffed on a riff that really lifted the show.

A Soho side street at midnight.
A sinister sense of sleaze.
Low life lurking
Old tarts smirking.
It was hard to feel at ease.

Waiting. Waiting.

I was queuing outside the Flamingo,
A twenty-deep line at the door.
Debris blowing.
Red lights glowing.
Was that shadowy shape a whore?

Waiting. Waiting.

A big, dark-coated bouncer
Was ignoring the crowd in line.
Wouldn't yield as
We appealed that
It was now past opening time.

Waiting. Waiting.

The Regent Shoes dark window
That I was stood beside.
Threw reflections
Of small sections
Of the gathering crowd outside.

Lurking. Lurking.

The people in line were alright.
All that they wanted was: IN.
Georgie Fame
Was why they came
But the periphery gave concern.

Lurking. Lurking.

Intent on the darkened shop window
I was squinting to get a sight
Of the tawdry,
Coarse and sordid
Denizens of the night.

Skulking. Skulking.

A shifty duo intrigued me
In an adagio dance.
He was scar-faced,
She just hard-faced,
Whispering dark romance.

Tangoing. Tangoing.

Then came a welcome reflection
It almost made me cheer.
Sleek, fur-fettered,
Five Lambrettas
Announced the Mods were here.

Circling. Circling.

Then there emerged from the shadows.
A businessman I'd not seen.
Far from relaxed.
Smile that seemed waxed.
He edged towards the scene.

Dealing. Dealing.

Perhaps it was this crowd's arrival
That the bouncer had waited for.
Banging a bolt
With a heave and a jolt
He finally opened the door.

Surging. Surging.

*

I could be wrong and suffering from suspect memories
But I recall the Flamingo Club as unlicensed premises.
A refreshment counter serving snacks was all that there would be.
And if you didn't fancy coke
It was strictly coffee or tea.
If, however, I'm correct then that might just explain
Why the air was always heavy with a whiff of something strange.
With nostrils twitching at each sniff beyond the opened door
I eased myself down narrow stairs
To the basement club below.

This club venue was different to most haunts we'd frequent
In pub back rooms or function halls where just a young crowd went.
The clientele at the Flamingo Club was consid'rably more mature.
Espec'lly at the midnight set
With its sinister allure.

I bought a Coke and settled in a space quite comfortably
And then I found six huge black guys were edging next to me.
From their sharp pressed shirts and their general stance I knew they had to be
A bunch of soldiers on a pass
From the US military.

Although they were all off duty and not in uniform
One of the guys amongst them was keeping his eye on form.
A certain air of vigilance implied he was 'in charge':
The small platoon's 'lootenant', or
Their 'captain' or their 'sarge'.

I gave a smile of greeting as I shuffled to make room.
And the gesture was acknowledged by the entire platoon.
'On a weekend pass, guys?' I enquired, to show I knew the score.
And they all laughed and clapped their hands
While the 'sarge' said, 'Aint that for sure!'

And, with the ice part broken now, I ventured to enquire:
'Have you caught the Blue Flames here or anywhere else before?'
And, again, 'sarge' was their spokesman saying, 'We've seen them back at base.'
'It sure is one cookin' band!'
Said another, moving his place.

'It's Georgie Fame who drives them on,' I told them eagerly.
'That husky voice just floats across his lovely Hammond B Three.'
'Did ya ever hear of Jimmy Smith?' one said, turning round.
'That cat plain invented
The Hammond organ sound!'

I didn't want to score a point by raising Wild Bill Davis' name.
But Louis Jordan's piano player had staked an earlier claim.
So I just slightly changed the tack and asked the whole platoon:
'And did you ever catch a guy
Called Jimmy Witherspoon?'

A soldier sucked his breath and told me: 'Times gett'n tougher'n tough!
 I make a lot of money,' I added. 'But I just keep spending the stuff!'
'Aint that the truth!' a soldier laughed and another said: 'Shawnuff is!'
And, hitting on this last remark
They began to take the piss.

'You get the blues, too, do ya "Shawny"?' a laughing soldier asked.
'He shawnuff does,' another claimed. 'When he gets his morning tasks.'
'Shawny' was much younger than the 'sarge's' other men.
He pulled a face and whimpered:
'Y'all pickin' on me again!'

Tall and lean but powerfully built, the kid looked just eighteen.
He clearly was their new recruit being painfully 'broken in'.
Well used to the friendly kidding now, as I could plainly see,
He turned away from the others
And addressed himself to me:

'Excuse me, sir, for askin' ya but I just gotta know:
Where'd ya get that coowal coat? Are you part of the show?'
I just laughed at this suggestion and said, 'The jacket's not unique.
It's Bleeding Madras striped cotton
From a small shop called Sportique.'

'Sportique!' The kid repeated and pencilled down a note.
While the others all watched in amusement as he carefully wrote.
'Ya planning to send a whole shipment out to Hogsville, Tenessee?'
A big guy asked him as a joke.
And I smiled in sympathy.

His int'rest in the gear I had on had given me a lift
But all at once I noticed that his attention began to drift.
I glanced across the club room at the focus of his gaze:
The crowd of Mods was shuffling in
And he was clearly fazed.

'And who exactly is that crowd of hipsters over there?'
'Where do they get their haircuts and the funky clothes they wear?'
I laughed and told him they belonged to an ultra-urban clan.
 'They're known as "Mods,"' I told him.
'And they're poseurs to a man!'

The club was getting crowded now. It was close to being full.
I ran the risk of being blocked out if I went for a quick re-fuel.
But I turned to the sergeant and asked if he'd mind saving me a place.
He took it as a military task
And stood two men in my space.

'Oh, by the way, my name's Sam,' he told me happily.
'It's good to meet you, Sam,' I said and shook hands formally.
'And I get the impression that you're this team's warrant officer in charge.'
The others really laughed at this.
And one said: 'Call him "sarge"!'

I slipped away, still smiling and feeling really pleased.
All sense of trepidation I'd had was absolutely eased.
I didn't make for the refreshment bar but decided I should head
For a quick trip to the bathroom
To relieve myself instead.

*

Although the club itself was packed, the gents' loo was quite quiet.
Mercifully, the troughs were free
With no hint of impending riot.

I stood myself at the furthest stall and carefully took my aim.
But, before I could start, the doors swung apart
And in walked Georgie Fame.

To say that I froze
Would not fully disclose
The throes of my poor body's spasm.

I could not perform
I suppose it's the norm.
But I wished I could sink in a chasm.

Pretending I'd done
I zipped up in one
And stepped carefully onto the tiling.

But then I could see,
He's just human like me,
And he seemed to be actually smiling.

So, stoically, I took a breath and, feigning nonchalance,
I tried not to choke as I actually spoke,
While giving a sideways glance.

'Any chance of "Night Train", George?' I asked him in a sweat.
He answered me quite amiably.
'It opens the second set!'

'That's good news,' I told him, feeling my poor toes curl.
'Though the Duke might prefer me to ask you for
"Happy Go Lucky Local"!'

I was gratified that Georgie laughed at this smart crack.
'Cos it seemed to me it could possibly be
Just a little bit too 'anorak'.

We rinsed our hands together then parted at the door.
But, when he'd gone, I turned around
To do what I'd come there for.

The bathroom was deserted still and I felt quite relaxed.
But, as I peed successfully,
The door opened at my back.

Stepping down I turned around
Then shivered at my core.
Coming in, pale and thin
Was a half of the adagio.

Though, somehow, his scarred face now
Filled me with less dread.
I could see, quite obviously
He was totally out of his head.

'What's my name? Georgie Fame!'
He was mumbling as he came.
'Georgie Fame! That's my name!'
I tried to scram in vain.

'Well, how y'doin', man?' He exclaimed,
As if we were old, old friends.
'Aintcha glad that y'came?'

'And what can I do
Tonight for you?
How much ya wantin' to spend?'

I tried to proceed
With the utmost of speed.
But the husk would just not let me be.

'Are ya losin' your voice?
Come on, just name yer choice.
And tell me whaddya need?'

'Well, I've got my whole health
And I'm working on wealth
So I think I'm okay for a while.'

Then the loo doors swung wide
And two Mods came inside.
Took in the scene and just smiled.

They were guys that I knew
From some Blues Rendezvous.
And they'd clearly met my friend before.

'Aloysius!' said one.
Clearly having some fun.
'That's lucky 'cos we wanna score.'

'Give me two Oxo cubes
Wrapped in silver foil tubes
And some of Hyde Park's best mown hay.'

We exchanged a few words
While the low life demurred.
Then I left them and went on my way.

But outside the swing door
In the dim corridor.
The adagio partner was lurking.

'Is my sugar lump in there?'
She asked, fing'ring her hair.
'Yeah,' I said, 'He's busy working.'

*

Struggling through the crowd around the refreshment counter
I was pleasantly surprised by another brief encounter.
It was Shoola, Southgate's local 'fool for rhythm',
And, under one arm he had
The usual Dobell's bag of collectable vinyl with him.

'Oochereeni!' was his enthusiastic greeting,
'What a place for a meeting.
You with the crowd? Come and join me.'
'I'm on my todd,' I told him.
'But I've joined a team of US military.'

'Spades?' he asked me excitedly.
'They'll love Mister Fame. Just wait and see
They'll understand what he's got.'
Then came his all-purpose endorsement:
'I tell you what!'

'Yes,' I agreed. 'They already know the score.
They've seen him back at the base before.'
And then I exclaimed as he caught me looking
At his current collection: 'They'd love this, too:
Jimmy Smith's "Home Cookin"'!'

'Hip kids!' was his parting suggestion.
As he struggled away through the heaving congestion.
To have followed would be a rebuff to Sergeant Sam,
Who was nobly defending my place in the crowd.
Tonight, he's 'my man!'

Back in my space and clutching a cold Coke, freshly brewed,
I thanked the Sarge for doing what he said he would.
I thanked as well the 'junior rank' who'd been standing guard.
And got a smile of welcome.
Saying: 'It weren't too hard!'

The club was now jam-packed, though folk were dancing at the back.
'Thanks a lot,' I said to the sarge. 'I really appreciate that.'
He smiled and nodded graciously then leaned in close to me.
'These "Mod" guys here,' he whispered.
'How do they tend to be?'

He threw a quick glance backwards to where the kid, 'Shawny',
Was mingling with the Lambretta crowd perfectly happily.
'We gotta keep an eye on the kid,' he murmured. 'Or he might.
Just say something out of line
And get into a fight.'

'They're pussy cats,' I told him. 'Unless you happen to be
From that other tribe called "Rockers". Then go carefully!
'But they'll love the fact that Shawny is so taken with their clothes.
So relax and stand well back.
Just see how it goes!'

The club was really heaving and a certain element
Was getting more than restless. Almost belligerent.
They'd been happy enough to hang around and wait when they first came
But now they were getting impatient and
Wanted to see Georgie Fame.

*

The capacity crowd
Was becoming quite loud
With a barrage of noisy complaint.

Some whistled and roared
Really giving what for.
With a notable lack of restraint.

'Is Georgie Fame here?
That's why we came here!'
You almost could hear them call out.

'Why are we waiting?
Anticipating,'
Was becoming a communal shout.

Would it be a no show?
The crowd just didn't know!
'Cos they hadn't seen him like me.

Yes, I knew for sure
That Georgie was here
And bided my time happily.

I took the chance
To just casually glance
At the mixture of folk who were there.

Such a wild sea of faces
From all known races
I was too mesmerised to feel scared.

Such a wide range of suits:
Some pin-striped, some zoots.
And the Mods in their hand-cut creations.

Chinese ladies in silk
Some complexions like milk.
It was truly the United Nations!

Grey beard jazz 'anoraks'
With their duffel bag packs.
And characters who looked pretty shady.

And, mumbling still,
Looking distinctly ill,
'Sugar Lump' clutching his lady.

'Is Georgie Fame here?
That's why we came here!'
It was almost an audible shout.

Then to deafening cheers
That damaged the ears.
On the stage, Rik Gunell sauntered out.

With a scotch in one hand
He welcomed the band
As clutching their horns they all came.

Then, drowned by the noise,
He said: 'Yes girls and boys,
Please welcome now, Georgie Fame!'

*

The band on the stand then began the Big Blow.
They biffed on a riff that really lifted the show.
The cheers in my ears were a piercing bellow.
And the call of them all was: 'Go, Georgie! Go!'

'Hey everybody,' came his scorching tone.
'Let's have some fun!
Y'don't live but once
And when yer dead yer done!
So …'

'Go, Georgie! Go!'
We know we're gonna love the show.
Don't care if we are young or ole
We're gonna Let The Good Times Roll!'

*

Sergeant Sam beside me was really in the groove
Both feet hopping.
Fingers popping.
He knew just how to move.

His soldiers, too, were smiling and shuff-er-ling their feet.
They all knew
Just what to do
When dancing to a beat.

On stage the hero, Georgie, his smile pressed to the mike
Was calling on
A saxophone
To play just what he liked.

And then it was the organ's turn to say a line or two
And effortlessly
That Hammond B Three
Just blew and blew and blew.

'But don't let any female,' came that voice again,
'Try to sell me cheap.
'Cos I've ….' The crowd took over his refrain:
<<Got fifty cents more than I intend to keep!>>

Oh, did those good times roll!
It was therapeutic for the soul.
And if you didn't feel it
You must have had a heart gone cold.

*

Looking round the club again at faces I could see,
The mix of people mingling there quite captivated me:
It seemed that all humanity
In its wide diversity

Was in the Flamingo Club tonight.
It really was an awesome sight.
Despite the darkness, I could see a smile on every face.
From 'Sugar Lump', dissolved now in his lover girl's embrace,

To 'Hooray Henry' trying to jive
With a lady twice his size.
Mods galore and US soldiers,
Low-life villains with padded shoulders.

This little slice of Soho life
Was an efficacious pill.
A hint of vice alive and rife
Can't hurt and never will.

A simple scene I witnessed as I looked around the room
Made me smile the wider and I nudged at Sergeant Sam.
I thought he would be gratified
To take a look at what I'd spied:

The Mods he'd been concerned about
Had somehow found some space
To do a little dancing
And, taking pride of place,
Was his raw charge, Shawny,
A big smile on his face.

They had formed a tight squeezed circle
To teach him how to do
The tricky footsteps to the dance
That initiates only knew.
And, contrary to the stereotype,
He wasn't initially getting it right.

But the point is, he was making friends
And the sergeant looked well pleased.
His concern had proved quite groundless.
And he was now at ease.
But one thing I instinctively knew:
Sam would have got those steps in two!

*

It was hard now to ever conceive
That this packed house had really believed
That Georgie Fame might let them down.

They were rejoicing at last in his voice
And the incredibly rhythmic choice
Of his small band's great big, fat sound.

The pulsating, gyrating, sensation
Of his Hammond B Three's explorations
Must have been echoing all over town.

But, here in the basement club
We were privileged to be at the hub
Of the music that was going down.

Georgie lived the life he loved
And he loved the life he lived.
It was obvious in his attitude.
He had so much real pleasure to give.

Yes, like the incredible mix of others
Making up this crowd.
I felt I wanted to raise my voice
And shout out good and loud:

'Thank you Georgie Fame.
I'm really glad I came!'

***

Those Flat Share Girls. (Oh, How They Laughed.)

... how their unforced joie de vivre
Enflamed a young man's heart like fever.

Oh, how they laughed, those flat share girls;
And how their laughter seemed to swirl,
Like tingling shards of ocean spray
Sun-caught on a summer's day.

Those bold, vivacious ingénues
Lived by the mantra: 'What's to lose?'
And had an aura, every one,
Of all-consuming, honest fun.

They'd ventured here from far and wide:
Cities and towns and countryside.
From Stockholm, Wellington and York.
From Michigan and County Cork.

Those Anne-Maries and Bernadettes
Had taken the gift that suffragettes
Had boldly fought for long ago:
'Ladies should be given a go!'

Like children on a playground trail
They'd come to play 'House' in Maida Vale.
Traded mum's ironing put away
For lives of domestic disarray.

With kitchen rotas on the wall
Anonymous backpacks in the hall.
They'd squeezed into bedsits, two a room,
In hope that adventure would find them soon.

But how their unforced joie de vivre
Enflamed a young man's heart like fever.
As, plund'ring the kitty for a round,
They laughed for joy at the life they'd found.

We used to seek them out in bars,
And drive them round in our fathers' cars.
But not as predators on the prowl,
That was neither our wish nor style.

It was their carefree game we craved.
We wanted to join them as they played.
We only hoped to be allowed
A place in their extended crowd.

We used to relish being there
As they tonged flick-ups in their hair.
Or carefully snipped at Mary Quants.
Those lovely, New Age debutantes.

Sipping cheap wine from rinsed jam jars,
They weren't exactly movie stars.
But affectionate girls and warm
Each with a different womanly form.

And, late at a party or on a date,
There would be cuddles to appreciate.
Wet, tongue-filled kisses; whispered words.
And a chance to fondle their breasts, of course.

Breasts and, just possibly, something more.
But not one was treated as a whore.
They were just friends who we adored.
As lovely, transient girls next door.

Misunderstandings and not betrayals.
Would cause a few romantic trials.
But after the salty tears were dried
No one remembered quite just why they'd cried.

But time moves on. All things must change.
And soon the sharing became re-arranged.
Relationships began to form
Or some of the girls just missed their homes.

The crowd began to drift apart
Visas expired. Some just moved out.
Others took boyfriends home to Perth
Or Manchester to meet their folks.

Nobody pricked the red balloon
It just deflated all too soon.
Those girls had brightened up my life.
Though I never took one as a wife.

*

How long ago were those innocent days?
How long ago? How far away?
I still receive the occasional card
From Adelaide or places less far.

'Hope this address still finds you,' they say.
'Remember Meg? Well, she passed away.'
Or: 'I'm a granny now, would you believe.
… D'you ever hear at all from Steve?'

I'm rarely in those parts of town
Where we used to hang around.
But when I am, I'm quite amazed
At just how little has really changed.

Huge great, five-floor houses still
Flower boxes on window sills.
Or tiny, terraced bijou homes.
That used to echo to 'Doo Ron Ron!'

And in Philbeach Gardens, if I'm there,
I can't resist to stand and stare.
And, at open gates, I might peep in

To look for wine-stained jam jars
Lying broken in the bin.

***

At Last

The crashing sea beside us turned, hissing, as we ran
And through the steaming darkness came heavy pellets of rain

Her fingers in my hand were slipp'ry
And her face and her hair were damp.
But the tears she had cried
Had been wiped to one side
And her green, Kohl-smudged eyes had both dried.

The night was far more than just humid
And the air that we breathed was like steam.
We had not run that far
But the small, beach-side bar
Was now faint as a long-fallen star.

We felt like creatures fleeing
From some wild and imminent storm.
The swelt'ring night air
Made the whole atmosphere
Claustrophobic; but we didn't care.

Then, breathlessly, we halted.
I took her in my arms.
Laughing now, she turned her face
To offer me her tongue.

Her breasts beneath that cotton shift
Were womanly and firm.
Pressed against my pounding chest
Her whole, young form was warm.

The talk in the bar had solved things.
Now the lingering doubts were gone.
All the fears of the past
Had been mist on a glass
We were going to be lovers at last.
At last!

*

The crashing sea beside us turned, hissing, as we ran
And through the steaming darkness came heavy pellets of rain
That built up to a torrent, flooding the sultry night.
We were now far away
From the bars by the bay
And their distant suggestion of light.

The phosphorescent ocean gave off an eerie glow
And we could really feel the surge of its wild undertow
But we were almost drowning in that torrential rain
As we fell, hand in hand,
On the now soaking sand
And her tongue found my mouth once again.

Her tongue was like succulent mango
Without that fruit's rubbery bone.
And, sucking to taste its rich flavour,
I could feel myself growing and growing.

Her dress peeled off like a peach skin;
Her underwear came the same.
Then she helped me slide out of my own things,
All the time whisp'ring my name.

How splendid it was to be naked
And to feel her wet breasts on my chest.
Though the bites that I gave her were gentle
She moaned like a spirit possessed.

As my wet mouth moved down her towards the moist split at her loin
I felt her fingers fondling the swelling of my groin.
Then, with renewed excitement, I licked the tangled hair
That concealed her cunt's lips.
And she raised up her hips
To allow me to lick where I cared.

Her beautiful vagina had a pungent marinade,
Like the salty skin of duck breast in a steaming cassoulet.
And, as my tongue continued in its intimate embrace,
She raised up her behind
From the base of her spine
And then squirted hot juice in my face.

I gasped with delight as I licked her
And then begged her to spray me again.
She rubbed at herself with her fingers
And made her juice gush like the rain.

She then slid herself round on my body
As the rain ricocheted from her hips
And knelt herself over my shoulders
To suck at my growth with her lips.

At last we were beginning to know each other well.
On cusp of consummation, when fevered passions swell
I licked again the moist gash that gaped above my face.
Then, turning her round,
To lie flat on the ground,
We moved to the final embrace.

With both bodies bare
I just fucked her right there.
And she wriggled and groaned
As my lingam, like bone,
Pummelled and pumped
In her scalding hot cunt.

I found myself practic'lly crying
As I bit at her hard-nippled breasts.
This was pure ecstasy
And the rain meant that we
Were as wet as that wild, raging sea.

I could feel myself reaching my climax
So I eased myself out of her loins
Her wet mouth opened wide
To invite me inside
And she sucked my hot cum as I sighed.

'Whoo!' she exclaimed as I licked her,
And she dribbled my juice on her breasts.
Then she poked out her tongue
And I tasted my cum
As I sucked at her like a ripe plum.

'You're a bit of a slut,' I said, 'aren't you?'
And she laughed as she slapped my behind.
But we found, as we teased,
Gasping at the hot breeze,
That the violent, wild rainstorm had eased

Just standing up was not easy.
We seemed to be weak at the knees.
And her now slimy breasts
Seemed to stick to my chest
As I gave her a tender caress.

'Love you so much,' I said softly,
And earned a wet kiss as reward.
The deed was now done
At last we'd become
Two hopeless, young lovers as one.

On that beach, beside the wild ocean,
Two figments frozen in space.
The ocean had us mesmerised
We craved its forgiving embrace.

I wrapped a damp arm around her
As we stood there for one moment more
Content to just gaze at the white surf
As it pounded itself on the shore

'Thank you,' I whispered quietly.
And , trembling, she fell into my arms.
Then I shared one more kiss,
Touched her moist clitoris
And squeezed one soft hand with both palms.

And, at last, hand in hand
Across the wet sand,
Of all the past doubts now quite free.
Unscared of death,
We both took a deep breath
And, like dolphins, dove at the sea.

* * *

The purpose of this next piece is not to give a resume of the career of a popular band of the time, (and long thereafter), but to give, in vignette snatches, a glimpse of an adventure I undertook juxtaposed against the feeling that I might be missing major events at the home I'd left behind. I kept hearing that London was 'Swinging'. Should I have stayed at home? — NO!

Where Was I?

.... far from the fuss and ballyhoo
I was on my way to Kathmandu.

I've lived a life without regret
And yet,
Child of the Sixties that I claim to be,
Where was I in sixty-three
When a wild new band called the Rolling Stones
Started shaking their black cat bones
To cast a kind of voodoo spell
While playing guitars 'like ringin' a bell'?

I was in the crowd at the old Marquee
To see
Alexis Korner and his wicked crew
Behind Cyril Davis as he sucked and blew
On an amplified tin sandwich while
Long John Baldry added his style
To create a sensational, punching mix
With a guy called Charlie guesting on stix.

And, as the punters yelled for more,
I saw
A big-lipped youth within the throng,
Three-button jacket and hair quite long;
And Shoola, there as usual, said to my ear:
'Give it a while and he'll be here!
He's in a band that's just been formed
And they're gonna take the scene by storm.

Don't, at the moment, have a name
But Fame
Is coming their way, just wait and see!
A New Sensation's what they'll be.
Ian Stewart on piano: very nice
And they cook their chords in Cajun Spice.
I caught them doing an interval set
And, tell you what: I'd put a bet

That, given the essential opening break,
They'll shake
This business to its core
They had the regulars shouting for more.
And that scrawny, little guy with the lips,
Tongue like a rattlesnake, hands on hips,
Really made his body move
While the boys in the band kept chugging a groove.

I'm a-tellin' you how it's a-gonna be:
Trust me!'
But when this prophecy came to be
I'm afraid the action bypassed me.

'Cos, far from the fuss and the ballyhoo,
I was on my way to Kathmandu!
While flames were leaping from Mick and Keef
My fire came from Thali on a banana leaf.

You might call it foolish vanity
To be
So upset that I can't swear
With hand on heart that I was there
When the 'Revolution' really began
Driven by this young, electric band.
I was squatting on a mat by a straw chai stall
While the boys were re-mixing Rock and Roll.

I'm almost ashamed to admit that I was
In Oz
Before I really heard the sound
That was spreading itself around.
Lost in the Northern Territ'ry
I was startled to hear the buzz of 'King Bee'.
As, camped beside a billabong,
A mate turned his transistor on.

And, in a burst of mad mayhem:
'It's them!'
He shouted jubilantly.
And turned triumphantly to me
As if it was him playing slide guitar
With the bottle neck of an old fruit jar.
Then, suddenly, the gum trees seemed
To be just part of an eerie dream.

I'd strayed a million miles from home
To roam
In search of who knows what or why.
I felt like hanging my head to cry.
But, then, the Outback called me back.
There was still a lot of baking 'Track'
That I had to tackle like a man
In a Holden 'Ute' with a billy can.

Adventure was my chosen game.
I came
In the hopes that life would be
A voyage of discovery.
It was pointless now to feel regret
For what I might be missing. Yet:
Would whatever I might find
Compare with what I'd left behind?

Trivial thoughts from a trivial mind
The kind
Of musings you'd expect to come
From a man whose life is a shallow sham!
But, curled in my bedroll, my poor brain
Ran over these thoughts again and again
I'd swapped a life of good times and booze
For spinifex and kangaroos!

Although it's true that at times today
I say:
'I've "mixed" with the icons of my age:
Sinatra shook my hand — from the stage

And, in that basement bar where Ronnie's began
Dexter Gordon called me "Man"!'
Heady stuff (or not, maybe),
But it meant an awful lot to me.

But when a band that I almost knew
Broke through
I wasn't there to watch the show
And feel the pandemonium grow.
Living on coral island beaches
With mango trees and fresh, ripe peaches,
Was all very well for a Young Romancer
But all I have left are the scabs of skin cancer!

And that's by no means all I missed.
Hear this:
Football's never meant a lot to me
But I'm moved by a sense of 'History'
And the English nation, with me away,
Was about to have its finest day!
The full throttle of that Wembley roar
Echoes still like the end of the war.

But while Bobby Moore was being held up high
On his teammates' shoulders
Where on earth was I?

*

In the desert of North Pakistan
Within the state of Baluchistan
There's a god-forsaken railway halt
Where overland travellers by default
Must skulk in the shadows to wait and wait
For a local train that's always late.
Two days late or sometimes three
It's like waiting at the whim of destiny.

Anyone who's done the desert 'Trip'
Will shudder and tremble at the lip
When someone whispers Nok-kundi's name
For it takes them back to that bleak terrain.
That arid, fly-blown, desolate place
Where the sun's like a blow torch on your face.
Flies up your nostrils in your ears.
The constant buzzing drives grown men to tears.

I'd been there for two whole days
Stranded by the train's delays.
Huddled in any shade I could find:
A fallen wall I could hide behind.
The only blessing was the company
Of two young Germans there like me.
Our paths had criss-crossed quite a lot
But I'd not seen them since the Ankor Wat.

They'd been amongst a few who'd dared
To sleep in the City while they were there.
At night each eerie ancient ruin
Lit only by the jungle moon

Was bathed in a magic, ghostly glow
As we explored them eagerly on tip toe.
Then stirred from our bed-rolls with a yawn
We dipped in the lake by the light of dawn.

Happier times than we currently shared
In that desert sun's relentless glare
And it wasn't just the unbearable heat:
There was absolutely nothing to eat.
A chai stall served up curried goat
In a thick grey sauce that burned your throat.
But that was all there was on Earth
And even the flies gave it wide berth.

Chapatis and water (from a drain?)
Sustained me, waiting for that damned train.
The torture led me to despair
That I was going to die right there.
But then at high noon on day three
A mirage appeared for all to see:
Two coaches of ancient rolling stock
Came trundling over the sand and rock.

Peasants on the roof with tin dustbins
They'd packed their worldly possessions in.
But first to dismount was a tall, young Sikh
Looking very dapper and sleek.
I wasn't at all surprised to see
That he made a beeline straight for me.
'And so, hello. Yes, my dear friend with the sunburnt face
Tell me what is your native place?'

'I'm from North London,' I told him with a smile.
(I was used to this question—and his cheeky style.)
'Well Mister Johnny North London,' he effused
With a handshake that I couldn't refuse.
'You are now a Champion of the World. Your might
Has filled Her Majesty with delight.'
I had no idea what he was talking about
But a couple of Kiwis came clambering out:

I knew the Kiwi guys quite well.
And they were very anxious to tell.
Both held one clenched fist up:
Saying: 'You bastards just won the World Cup!'
Helmut and Gunter were standing nearby
And looked as if they were going to cry.
'Is this the truth?' they shouted in woe
And the Sikh held up his radio.

'It's hot from the airwaves, my dear friend.'
And he insisted on shaking my hand again.
'Vembley and Nok-kundi,' hissed Gunter in despair.
'Zere are hell-holes everywhere.'
But he laughed and shook my hand for sport.
While the Sikh slapped my shoulder with the retort:
'Calls for a snifter, wouldn't you say?
What time's the local open today?'

Every one of us laughed out loud
And Mister Singh became one of the crowd.
He asked us please to call him 'Charlie' and
Shook us all formally by the hand.

A point he could not possibly have missed
Was that we each wore Sikh bangles at our wrist.
It marked us as Gurdwara Bums
But our new companion didn't let on.

The Kiwi guys, it soon transpired
Had met the Germans long before.
And I had got to know them well
At Bangkok's Thai Song Greet Hotel.
We'd hung out at a local bar
With black GIs on R&R
And I'd met them last at another stop:
The city of Kabul's notorious 'Long Drop'.

So now we were six lost souls
Waiting for the two coach train to roll.
There'd be at least a four-hour delay
Before the thing got underway.
Then across the border to Iran
We'd be dumped at a city called Zahedan.
But at least there'd be some shelter there
And some halfway decent culinary fare.

*

When I got to Zahedan
My plan
Was to head straight through the Arab lands
Not even stopping at Isfahan.
I'd 'done' the bazaar and the mosques before
And now I craved my homeland shore

I might stop in Istanbul again where, across the Bosphorus, waited
Europe. I felt quite elated.

Soon I would be home again
And then
I'd find exactly what had gone on
In the three long years that I'd been gone.
Not much, I was inclined to think.
A string of same old parties where drink
Had left the gang half blind.
This is what I'd left behind.

I wondered if my trip had changed me.
Strangely,
I really didn't think it had.
I was still a naïve, trusting lad.
Confusing dreams with real ambition
I needed to sort out my position.
To take a firm control of fate
And not just sit around and wait.

But soon enough that time would come,
Back home,
When I could take a stock of my life
For now, I simply had to survive
And cross more burning, barren sand
Before I reached my Promised Land.
I found myself just looking
Forward to my dear mum's cooking.

And sleeping in my own soft bed
Instead
Of the bedroll smelling of sweat
And my soiled and torn mosquito net.
But now I'd reached the final stretch
I found the foolish sense of regret
That plagued me in an earlier day
Had quite completely gone away.

I didn't regret what I had missed because
I had the mem'ries of 'Where I Was'!

***

What Did You Do?

When 'The Myth of the Rainy Night'
Turned sour on you.

You were there, too,
Weren't you?
You were out on the road
When the Sixties explo-
-sion was new.
Weren't you?

We thought that we
Had found the key.
Because we both came of age
With a wonderful rage
To be free.
Didn't we?

But what did you do
When 'The Myth of the Rainy Night'
Turned sour on you?
And the dream of a Brave New World
Did not come true?

What did you do?
What did you do?

We lived as though the whole world
Was there for just our sake.
Unprecedented freedom was there

For us to take.
Until we felt the Helter Skelter break
And we were shaken in its wake.

Then, where did you run?
When the seam
Of that naïve dream
First came undone?
And the War
Of which we were never sure
Was left unwon.

Where did you run?
Where did you run?

You took a train
Home again
To the life that you'd known
In the warmth of your own
Penny Lane.
Still unchanged.

Picked up the thread
Of the life that you'd led.
Began a career
As a dark-suited her-
-o instead.
Company man
On a corporate plan.

So where did they go,
All of those 'Wild Children' that we used to know?
If you saw them in the street now
Would you even say: 'Hello'?

Where did they go?
Where did they go?

*

What did you do
When 'The myth of the rainy night'
Turned sour on you?
And that dream of a brave new world
Did not come true?

I did it, too.
I did it, too!

* * *

Jack Kerouac On the Road:
'God was gone; it was the silence of his departure. It was a rainy night. It was the myth of the rainy night!'

The Tempest William Shakespeare:
Act 4 Scene 1 Miranda
    'O wonder!
    How many godly creatures are there here!
    How beauteous mankind is! O brave new world,
    That has such people in't.'

Charles Manson. *His assertion that the innocuous Lennon & McCartney song,* **Helter Skelter**, *was in some weird way a mission statement for his family:*
    'It says "Rise!" It says "Kill!" Why blame it on me? I didn't write the music.'

---

*'**Penny lane** is in my ears and in my eyes*
    There, beneath the blue suburban skies'
Lennon And McCartney 1968

Van Morrison Wild Children
'We were the Wild Children.
Born nineteen forty five
When all the soldiers came marching home
Love looks in their eyes.'

First To Go

So all the lads hired morning coats
And turned up with silk cravats at their throats.

I got back from my travels just in time
To catch the first of the wedding bells chime.
An old mate, Gerry, had decided to quit
The merry go round. He'd done his bit
Of passing the 'package' in musical chairs.
Breaking his heart over wild affairs.

There had come a time when the music stopped
And, in the scramble to stay on top,
He'd caught sight of himself in a looking glass
Holding a parcel too good to just pass
And realising the gift that he'd got
He took a deep breath and whispered: 'Why not?'

Most of the crowd were delighted, of course.
Though some couldn't think of anything worse.
P'raps they foresaw that this was the start
Of the 'old gang' gradually drifting apart.
Word got around by a spurious chance
Naming the chosen bride and groom's dance:

'When a Man Loves a Woman' by Percy Sledge.
Some of whose lyrics were close to the edge:
Particularly a line that's quite profound:
'Turns his back on his best friend if he puts her down!'
For there'd been an ugly row at a party
Like a scene from the movie 'Marty'

When a mate followed Gerry to the bog
Pissed and hissing: 'She's a dog, Gerry. Just a dog!'
Jealousy, of course. But I'm glad to say
He was man enough to apologise next day
And was as delighted as most
When his invitation turned up in the post.

So all the lads hired morning coats
And turned up with silk cravats at their throats.
The ladies, too, turned out in style
With ridiculous hats and vivacious smiles.
The mother of the bride dabbed happy tears
While we struggled with hymns we'd not sung for years.

The reception was a quite lavish affair.
I was amazed at the number of guests who were there.
Family, of course, mixing well with the crowd.
The predictable uncle who became overloud.
The best man gave a hilarious speech
Which brought almost everyone up on their feet.

For dancing they'd hired a great 'wedding band'
Who seemed more than happy to stay on the stand.
So we danced and performed and generally had fun
Until time for the lovebirds to make their run.
With old boots on the bumper of the grey Silver Cloud,
Their chauffeur struggled to steer through the crowd.

But even after the new weds were gone
The bride's father's party went on and on.
Gerry had paid for an open bar
So we all said: 'Cheers, Jezza. You're a real star!'
We didn't have very far to get home
'Cos we'd all got bookings in a hotel room.

The hotel wasn't that far away
So most made the Kings Head at lunchtime next day.
Silk frocks and morning suits back on their racks
Some of us suffering from pains in our backs.
It had been a very special occasion.
And we wished Gerry well in his new situation.

But I thought we all seemed a little subdued.
As if some concern were dampening our mood.
Within the large crowd were now several 'pairs'.
Couples who'd quit the 'musical chairs'.
One couple there was already engaged.
And others were not very far from that stage.

It was an inevitable process of life
That couples became man and wife.
And when you look to take a spouse
You need a deposit for the house.
So friends of old were now keeping low,
Saving for a flat or a bungalow.

The loose and easy camaraderie
Was changing imperceptibly.
For most of us, with intimacy
Came new responsibility.
No more rolling round in cars
Looking for entertainment bars.

Things weren't going to be the same.
We'd soon be playing a different game.
I wasn't really that upset.
But I hadn't met my partner yet.

* * *

A Sermon On A Mount

Was it John the Baptist who
Had so little else to do
That he took himself to the wilderness
To seek redemption and confess?

I used to be a young Boy Scout
Is that a surprise?
I used to wear a woggle
And swear to not tell lies.
I didn't mind the dib dib dob,
The bullshit and the bob a job.

'Akela' of the wolf cubs
In time became our 'Skip'.
And even though I realised
That it wasn't really hip

For years and years I stuck it out:
The job of being a young Boy Scout.

*

It was the summer camps that kept me!
The wonderful only chance
To throw myself at the countryside
And soak up its romance.

I knew that out there fields were waiting
And thickets of twisted gorse.
The woods, so dark and mysterious.
The farmer on his horse.

These were encounters quite unknown
To a boy who came from a city home.

All year I'd long for wild heathland
Wood pigeons cooing at night.
And dusk settling over the meadows.
Wild rabbits fleeing in fright.

And what boy living 'neath neon lights
Ever sees the stars at night?

Yes, the countryside was a different world
A world I loved to see.
So tying the occasional knot or two
Meant that it might be.

*

And so it was that one fine day,
As the sixties slipped away,
I decided to take a two-week stroll
Starting off at Hadrian's Wall.
An easy project, some might say:
I set out to do the Pennine Way.

I found a rucksack tucked away
Paid to join the YHA.
Wainwright's journal seemed a plan,
He was deemed to be the man.
An Ordnance Survey map or two
And a pair of sturdy crepe sole shoes.

And that was it: I had the gear.
Now I could just disappear.
Was it John the Baptist who
Had so little else to do
He took himself to the wilderness
To seek redemption and confess?

Well, with me it was the air;
The smell of heather wafting there.
Wainwrights' sketches spurred me on
'Til I felt mild delirium.
Trickling streams and waterfalls.
Some ruined castles in the hills.

Hadrian's Wall was just a dream.
You could see what must have been.
Housman on his 'Heaving Hill'
Sensed Roman soldiers lurking still?
Well, that exactly caught my mood
Gazing out above Twice Brewed.

Day two saw me fare less well:
What path to take was hard to tell.
Though the map showed dotted lines
On the ground there were no signs.
And soon I'd wandered so off course
I was to my chest in gorse.

But, still, ling'ring at a stile
Made the effort well worthwhile.
Splendid hills I gazed upon.
Untamed flowers all around.
Cows and flocks of baa-ing sheep
Who'd run and climb and turn and leap.

Walking makes me want to sing
It spurs me in my wandering.
Not 'Val de rah' but other songs
That help to make the path less long.
A current hit song of the day
Came to me as I went my way:

'Goin' up to the spirit in the sky.
'S where I wanna go when I die.
When I die and they lay me to rest …'
Well, you prob'ly know the rest.
Clapping hands to keep the time
Things were going pretty fine.

Not another soul to see.
Total silence. Only me.
Cows at hedgerows chewed their cud.
Mooing lightly as they did.
Others knowingly shook their head.
Saying: men in anoraks are mad.

Not that I was sporting one.
I had gone for a waxed blouson
That Aquascutum was clearing.
It matched the chinos I was wearing.
So elated I could die:
'Gonna recommend me to the Spirit in the Sky!'

This was what I'd hoped to find
When I'd left my life behind.
Crags and scars and sheltered nooks.
Tors and tumbling hillside brooks.
The trek was not at all a chore.
My back was strong and my feet weren't sore.

All that would change when I reached day four.

*

Such bleak, dark menace lurks in rain
That it makes you want to think again
About paradise and life's great plan.
To ponder on the fate of man.
I'd arrived by bus at the hostel door
About seven-fifteen the night before.
And Scarndale Burn was a sheltered vale
A peaceful hamlet on the trail.

But ten o'clock the following day
Saw rolling clouds of ominous grey.
Though 'Nah,' the surly warden said,
It looked to me like rain ahead.

Not more than a mile along the track
I really felt like turning back.
Although the rain was still at bay.
I was cursing at the day.

The damp and clammy hillside mist
Was slapping like an open fist.
Completely gone was the slightest trace
Of path or 'way' or shelt'ring place.

The hope of Langdon Beck grew faint
Unless I found a bus or train.
But what would be the chance of that?
Then something awful made me start.

A dead sheep lay there on its side.
Its wool-cased stomach open wide.
Beset by fat and buzzing flies
Maggots crawling in its eyes.

Shudd'ring as I gave it berth
I tried to hurry on the path.
To call it 'path', though, makes it sound
As though some footprints marked the ground.

There were none. Not one at all.
No trampled grass to call a trail.
No acorn sign to point the way.
No ray of sunlight in the day.

Just a steady upward slope
Where dark mist said: 'abandon hope!'
This was getting really bad.
I clenched my fists and shook my head.

Was it foolish venturing on?
Should I simply turn around?
Wainwright's journal pencilled in
A tiny hamlet with an inn.

But I couldn't say with certainty
That I was near where I should be.
I hadn't seen, 'cos of the dark,
A single one of his landmarks.

'Val de ree. Val de rah. Ha ha ha ha ha ...'

I wasn't in the mood to sing.
I wanted more than anything.
To get myself away from here.
With p'raps a pint of local beer.

What a wretched awful day.
I wasn't even sure which way
That dead sheep full of maggots lay.
But I pressed on: I couldn't stay.

So, breathing deeply, bowing head
I tried to keep a steady tread.
Until it struck me that, by now,
The mist was actually low lying cloud.

A lashing rain began to fall.
I couldn't see a thing at all.
The pelting torrent in my face
Seemed to be like death's embrace.

Then blind panic made me fall.
I stumbled forward and then rolled.
A sudden fear of injury
Took an awful hold of me.

I stood up slowly. Found no sprain
Thought that I could breathe again.
But the worst was yet to come:
I didn't know where I'd come from.

What was forward? What was back?
I'd quite completely lost the track.
Consuming terror clutched my groin.
Worst fear that I'd ever known.

I was in the wilderness!
No food. No shelter and quite lost.
I simply did what a million score
Had done before me, I'm quite sure.

I looked towards the hidden sky.
Stretched out my hands, let out a cry:
'Oh, Lord. Please, for heaven's sake.
Give this mortal fool a break!'

Though total silence was His reply
I still felt a presence in the sky.
I took a breath and tried again
Struggling in the pelting rain:

'I've never been a man to plead
But help me in my hour of need'.
Silence still and pounding rain.
But I know my plea was not in vain.

I sensed above me in the cloud
A wise old man who laughed out loud.
Hands on hips and feet apart.
Saying: 'Look at you, you stupid tart.'

He didn't say another word.
But I had heard what I had heard.
And all at once, just yards away
I perceived a different day.

The cloud was lifting gradually.
Still no sun but I could see.
A blind man healed will rub his eyes
And look around him in surprise.

Well, that's how it now was with me.
Surprised to see what I could see:
Scarndale Burn in its quiet vale
Was what awaited on my trail.

The mist had made me loop a loop.
Like a school kid with a hoop.
My 'wilderness' was a picnic spot.
Primrose Hill was more remote.

And there was a whisp'ring in my ear.
Saying: 'Gertcha now. Get out of here
I'm a very busy man.
Working on my Master Plan.'

I checked in at the local inn.
A modest place but welcoming.
And when I'd washed myself and dried
I had a beer and homemade pie.

Then there was something else to do.
An urgent mission to see through.
I strolled round to His local house.
A tiny chapel filled with flowers.

I chose a waiting wooden pew
And did the thing I had to do.
With both hands clasped and eyes shut tight.
I said the words I thought were right:

'Thank you, God, for helping me.
There's daylight now and I can see.
Maybe I've been too headstrong
The path I've chosen could be wrong.

But I'm holding on to this new thought:
A man who ignores what he's been taught
Isn't "hip" and isn't "cool".
He's just an arrogant young fool!

Thank you and amen.'

I lingered in the church a while.
And, at the door, I gave a smile.
I felt like clean, dry woollen socks
As I put a fiver in the box.

*

Every single good Boy Scout
Who's sworn to not tell lies.
Will tell you that you don't give up
If you want to win a prize.

So day five morning: dib dib dob.
I was up and at the job.
A gentle sunshine warmed the day
And Wainwright and I were on our way.

'Going up to—Val de rah. Val de rooh!'

* * *

By Starlight

But for all that we share
I might just as well talk to the stars.

By starlight
There should be so much to say.
Together,
All of life's strains far away.
So many secrets,
Intimate secrets.
Things we don't whisper for play.
But, for all that we share,
I might just as well talk to the stars.

In daylight
There isn't time to explain
The feelings
That evanesce in our brain.
Indistinct feelings.
Poorly formed feelings,
Fading too fast to retain.
But confiding in you
Is like trying to talk to the stars.

*

So we live our lives alone,
Making friends of a kind
With gestures and signs.

Our real selves remain unknown.
Held in prison behind
The walls of our mind.

*

By starlight,
Wrapped in the night's soothing calm,
The darkness
Eases my soul like a balm.
Machines entertain us.
They feed us and drain us
Until I could scream with alarm.
But escaping with you
Makes me feel I'm alone with the stars.

* * *

Blayden Thane

.... what became
Of Blayden Thane?

I remember,
With fragments of total recall,
Exploring England,
The summer when I first left school.

And I remember,
while drifting through small, market towns,
Feeling my childhood
Was done but my life not begun;

And that's when I came
Upon Blayden Thane.

     *

I came by train
To Blayden Thane
In an ambivalent mood.
I strolled each lane
In Blayden Thane
Where woodpigeons cooed
And cows mooed as they chewed.

In that perfect English June
There were wild hawthorn blooms
Festooned
On fences.

And on warm afternoons
Rich, sensuous perfumes
Consumed
My senses.

A perfect stillness
Was settled on those summer lanes,
As if a solstice
Were marking my own season's change.

And how my mind raced,
Creating an ambitious Life Plan,
While sipping cider
Outside the old inn on the green.

Watching duckweed fronds
On dark brown ponds.

My life took aim
In Blayden Thane.
It was a vital, new game.
Purpose and aim
In Blayden Thane

When fortune and fame
Seemed mine to claim.

*

But you know how time slips by
And the things you meant to try
Just lie
Unconquered.

So my own life drifted by.
The great ambitions just died.
Untried.
Unlonged for.

Without a murmur
I'd soon put myself up for rent.
In hired labour
My untried potential was spent.

I let convenience
Take on the reins of my fate.
Was all so easy
To let circumstances dictate.

I had lots of fun
But got nothing done.

        *

Then one weekend
I'd been staying with a friend
Who had moved out of town
And invited me down.
But, when heading back home,
I drove down a wrong turn
And a new motorway
Took me badly astray.
Into great greystone slabs
Of ugly pre-fabs.
Which endlessly
And bendlessly
Grew all around
A grotesque new town.
And then:

A minor turning
I caught on a roundabout sign.
Invoked a yearning
From deep in the back of my mind.

I slowed the car down
And started repeating the name.
Looking out all around
To try and find something the same,

For I'd come back again
To Blayden Thane.

*

But things had changed
In Blayden Thane.
Looking round I was appalled.
Nothing remained
Of Blayden Thane:
Just a concrete wall
Of urban sprawl.

Oh, what became
Of Blayden Thane?
Seeing it made my heart sore.
Where there'd been lanes
In Blayden Thane.
There were cut-price stores
With plate-glass doors.

I remembered
That sensuous hawthorn in bloom.
The blown aroma
Of that wild hedgerow's perfume.

And I remembered
Just how very young I'd once been.
Drunk on dry cider
Outside the old inn on the green.

Which, I saw from the car,
Was now a disco bar.

Oh, what became of Blayden Thane?
I saw it all in a glance.
The same that came
Of my life's aims:
They just stood no chance
'Gainst circumstance.

And where had flown
My only Youth?
Could I not claim it again?
Sat there alone
I was shown the truth:
It was gone like the lanes
That were once Blayden Thane's!

* * *

Complete

*Slowly, imperceptibly,
I started thinking, just maybe,
I'd found the other half of me.*

And then finally came
The day when I said:
'I am incomplete.
It's time I was wed!'

Up 'til that point
I'd not understood
What my loyal friends meant
(Though I'm sure they meant good),

When, touching my shoulder,
They'd lower their tone,
And say: 'It must be lonely
To live all alone!'

'Lonely?' I'd say
And then laugh out loud.
'One is good company.
Two's just a crowd.'

And I meant what I said,
It was not just for face.
I enjoyed having total
Control of my place.

There'd been ladies I'd known
As more than just friends
Who'd helped me to pass
Some quite pleasant weekends.

It was lovely to feel
Them beside me in bed;
Naked and warm
Underneath the bedspread.

But I felt no regret
When the weekend was done
To jump in the car
And drive them back home.

And then to return
At late evening to find
The flat, still and silent,
Was totally mine.

To do just as I chose,
To play music or not.
To just sit and stare,
(Which I did quite a lot),

Was so utterly perfect
I tingled with joy
And considered myself
The luckiest boy.

I'd enjoyed the brief pleasure
Of their company.
But now I was free to
Just take care of me.

It's not that we'd quarrelled
Though sometimes I wished
They wouldn't complain
About bones in the fish.

Or tell me the prime
Fillet steak I'd prepared
Was too rich with garlic
And a bit over-rare!

(When I went round theirs
For weekends to stay.
The best they could do
Was a cold takeaway!)

And none of them cared
For my musical choice:
Miles Davis' mute flugel
Or Chet Baker's voice.

And I suppose one meant well
When she asked me to play
Her CD of Barbara
Murders Broadway.

*

But that's all by the by!
Let's get back to my theme:
I found myself wond'ring
Was life all it seemed?

Was I just a half person?
Not totally whole?
And should I, p'raps, re-think my life
Before I grew too old?

At just about this time,
Coincidentally,
I'd become involved with a lovely girl
Who seemed quite fond of me.

And, true to all the proven
Romantic recipes,
We very soon discovered
She was chalk to my old cheese.

Never was a couple so
Diametrically opposed.
But every single thing I lacked
She had down to her toes.

She talked of a 'skill set'
Where I would call it 'talent'.
I would dream where she would plan.
It should have been abhorrent.

But I noticed on an early date that,
When she ordered fillet steak,
She liked the blood oozed on her plate.
And asked for lots of garlic.

And, when it came to buying the round,
She wasn't one to mess around.
She liked her gins poured large, I found,
With just a splash of tonic.

Slowly, imperceptibly,
I started thinking, just maybe,
I'd found the other half of me.

*

It comes as quite a sobering shock
To find yourself forced to take stock
Of the life you'd lived quite happily.
It left me dazed
And slightly fazed.

But, from the outset, it was clear
That this new young lady was here
To stay. And meant to take good care of me.
I felt quite glad.
It wasn't bad.

She was a 'Dub' from Dublin town.
She'd come to London to look around.
And it seemed she liked what she had found.
(I mean the city,
Not just me!)

I don't know just what news she had sent
To the Dublin family
But I daresay they included
Some snippets about me.
And, quite early on in the relationship,
Unexpectedly,
Her father arrived on a visit;
And we got on famously.

Or so I thought.
But I found that, on the sly,
He'd whispered to her anxiously:
'Please find a younger guy!'
A comment that was fair enough
Because, the fact is that I
Was almost the same age as him.
Did he think I was going to die?

But it seems that he relented
Or, maybe, just gave in.
Because when he went back home he left me
A litre of Cork Dry Gin.

So that was the dowry paid in full.
We drank it all one night.
And she said, while quite sober still,
'Would you like me to move in?'
And I said: 'Oh, alright.'

*

And that was my life changed for good:
Irrevocably!
Irredeemably!
No longer would
I be able to bask in total silence.
The way I previously could.

But it really wasn't bad at all
To have her company.
In my bed
And in my head.
It was good for me.

So, in my 'penthouse' two-bed flat,
I was happy to cohabit, but
A Catholic girl's not having that!
She made it very clear.

Although she acted with restraint,
Never voicing a complaint,
'Is we is or is we ain't?'
Hung always in the air.

So time came, eventually
When I asked her, or she told me
(I can't remember precisely),
'Let's get married, dear.'

*

Then, in Dublin's fair citee,
Cathedral bells chimed mightily
And, dressed like a fairy from a Christmas tree,
She marched down the aisle to link with me.
An organ played majestically.
A small choir sang angelically.
We both said: 'Yes' emotionally
And life as I'd known it ceased to be.

       *

That was twenty years ago.
It's worked out very well.
We're still in love,
As friends can tell.
But, more than that,
We seem to gel.

And, seeing life from her perspective,
Has given my own life a new objective.
And I try my best to never moan
That our lovely home is not our own.

We share it almost endlessly
With low-life scum on the teevee.
Thieves and rapists.
Killers, too.
Philandering couples,
Families who
Stand and scream
At high volume
In the centre of our living room.

But I've got headphones close at hand
For when the time comes I can't stand
Another hysterical dispute.
I can slip them on and listen to Zoot
Or Vivaldi or Beethoven
While dinner's cooking in the oven.

Yes, our life is really very sweet
And a thought that I often now repeat
Is: 'Living on my ownsome, way back when,
It must've been so lonely then!'

***

They Moved Like Dancers

... From the damp, dark nowhere
A laughing couple sprung.
The essence of life seemed within them
And in an instant I was young.

The final set at Ronnie's
Could have been a slight mistake.
I had work next morning
And it was more than late.
A cold rain stabbed my face like wire.
Suddenly I felt very tired.

But, caught upon an impulse
That I couldn't quite explain,
I set out on a detour
Despite the icy rain.
Before the night bus to my door
I felt a strange need to explore.

Although the streets of Soho
Were still familiar lanes,
A host of village landmarks
No longer now remained.
Places once my stamping ground
In the days when I still got around.

I was pleased to see Bar Italia
Still looking much the same
As it did when, a long, long time ago,
A schoolmate and I came
And, aged about fourteen,
Had my first 'froffy coffee' from a Gaggia machine.

Yes, Bar Italia was surviving still
But their long-time neighbour had closed his till:
Jimmy the Greek was now long gone
But the mem'ry of his place lives on:
Down and round the narrow stair
To the worst food you'd find anywhere!

But it wasn't Jimmy's 'culinary flair'
That brought his patrons to eat there.
And his was not the only place
That had now become a vacant space.
The music venues I once knew
Had, all of them, long vanished, too.

Not the venues of today
Where ten thousand people queue and pay
To watch their idols on a giant screen.
That is not my sort of scene.
I still prefer, by far,
To catch my heroes at the bar.

I struggled to remember now
Precisely where these music bars
And members' clubs had been.
But I'd seen lots of future stars
Half-hidden in the gloom
Of a dark and smoky basement or a pub back room.

It was sad to see these places gone.
As, wearily, I trudged along.

My steps became more weary
As, wet with wintry rain,
I turned left into Greek Street,
Where I knew not much remained.
Of what had, in my youth, once been
A rich and vibrant music scene.

Although the street lights sparkled
I peered in vain to see
A doorway that might mark the spot
Where Les Cousins used to be.
There Bert Jansch and Davy Graham
Had plucked their ways to cultish fame.

John Martyn, too, had played there
To rapturous applause.
To dwell on that scene's passing
Made me wearier because
It wasn't just the venue gone:
The troubadours themselves had flown.

Vanished venues.
Darkened lights.
Forgotten heroes
Long-closed sites.

At each turning as I trudged my way
There lurked mem'ries of olden days.
A sense of loss in the bitter cold
Was making me feel very old.

Then, all at once and suddenly, I was startled by a sound.
Like wild birds fleeing from their nest on a woodland ground.
I looked at the narrow laneway from where the noise had come
And from the damp, dark nowhere
A laughing couple sprung.
The essence of life seemed within them.
In an instant, I was young.

*

They moved like dancers,
Perfectly in time.
His bright, wide eyes entranced hers.
Their union was sublime.

Though hardly more than walking
Their tread was synchronised.
Without even talking,
Their spirits harmonised.

His hand on her left shoulder
Was urgent in its grip.
As if at any moment
He was going to lift her with a skip.

Their shapes threw several shadows
From the dim street lights nearby.
Dark shades shifting sideways
Sliding silently while I
Moved quietly behind them
Struggling to keep dry.

Then, step-ball-change together,
Their movement took new form.
As if, at last, untethered,
He spun her in a turn.

And they turned like tumblers;
Branches in a breeze.
Twisting and not stumbling,
With such acrobatic ease.

Then Soho's rain-damp pavements,
Glistening for the pair,
Became the empty ballroom of
Rogers and Astaire.

*

Captured in this couple's dance
Was the essence of romance.
The passion that ignites the soul
Whether the body is young or old.

So what that I'd seen Roland Kirk
A half century ago.
Or stood and cheered at Elkie Brookes
Fronting Vinegar Joe.

Or Frankie Miller with Brinsley Schwarz;
The Morrisey Mullen band, of course.
I'd had my time of 'being there',
I'd been around and had my share.

But now it was this couple's turn
To enjoy the delight of being young.
And in their foolish dance routine
They demonstrated what I mean.

Where had they just come from?
What dark, clandestine lair?
Surely some new rendezvous
Of which I was unaware.

The world can't thrive on mem'ries.
New action must evolve.
Around these lovers, dancing now,
The future would revolve.

*

Their dance continued
With a perfect pas de deux.
He led the movement momentr'lly
Then demurred to her.

Spinning sideways slowly
Then stepping back again
They were more bewitching
Than Nureyev and Fonteyn

They laughed like children
Playing a foolish game.
Jumping high and vaulting
As if waltzing in a flame.

*

I slowed my pace to near standstill
To better view the pair.
And, watching, I could not be sure
If they knew I was there.
But one thing was quite certain:
They didn't really care.

Then, as quickly and impulsively
As when they first appeared,
A new dark turning swallowed them
And they were no longer there.

I could, of course, have followed them
Down their pitch black lane.
But I was not some midnight stalker
Out prowling in the rain.

A shadowy glimpse was all I gained
Of their departing forms.
But their brief presence left me
Feeling positive and warm.

They moved like dancers,
Heading for the wings.
Content that their performance
Had been a wondrous thing.

*

The route of my original plan
Would now have taken me
Sharp left, then right up Poland Street
To pass the old Marquee.

Where once Cyril Davis and LJB
With Alexis Korner, guitar on his knee,
Had been amongst the heroes
That I used to queue to see.

'Who cares?' I thought. 'I'll head for the night bus outside the 100 club
And be in bed by three!'

***

When an old mate dies

Completely Gone

Ta ta y'old bastard. Safe journey on your trip!

'Fucking good riddance, too,' you say
As the wooden casket slides away.
And his widow laughs 'cos she knows he, too,
Would say the same if it was you.
But this brave jesting can't disguise
The red rim round your salt stung eyes.

The good, old mate you've known so long
Has now just quite completely: gone!

But it's not when the brown box slips t'wards the flames
('Cos you're too busy trying to remember the names
Of the sea of old faces who've appeared from the past)
That you comprehend this is definitely the last
You'll ever see of your old friend.
That his life on earth has reached its end.

You hope a deaf'ning noise will come from deep within that box
Of his fists punching desp'rately, giving loud and angry knocks.
And his gruff voice demanding: 'Is this somebody's joke?
You're not turning me into ashes and black smoke!'
But you listen out in vain.
You'll not hear his voice again

You try to understand the concept of the words 'mortal remains'
For that is all the plywood box before you now contains.
Just a transient encasement provided at his birth.
A flesh and blood container for his soul whilst here on Earth.
An empty shell, no more
The spirit that once drove it has now gone on before.

It came as a surprise to learn, with years of knowing him,
That all that time he'd nurtured a secret 'favourite hymn'.
It was: 'Onward Christian Soldiers' and though not at all obscure
You almost asked his widow: 'Are you absolutely sure?'
You couldn't ask your mate.
It was just too late.

You still wish you'd suggested that everybody sing
'Over the Rainbow' 'cos above everything
He hated that song with unreasonable force.
And you'd have just loved to sing yourself hoarse.
To hear a final growl.
Or, perhaps, a strangled howl.

'So, what on earth went wrong this time?' You lamely ask of him.
As you join in the chorus of that rousing 'favourite hymn'.
'We all know that you've suffered from some nasty turns before
But cussed willpower always brought you back from death's dark door.'
But no explanation comes.
'Cos he's quite completely: gone!

No, it's not in the funeral parlour at all
That you realise an impenetrable wall,
An unyielding obstruction has emerged between you
And the constant companion that you knew.
He hasn't just moved on.
He's quite completely gone.

It's in the months that follow you start to realise
What is really meant by the expression 'his demise'.
No more the quick phone call saying: 'Just to let you know
I'm around tonight if you want to buy that drink you owe.'
You will telephone in vain.
He'll not get them in again.

And, standing in that same old bar with the usual 'rentacrowd'
When a tosspot that you've known for years starts getting overloud,
He won't be there to scowl and share that weary skyward glance.
There's only you to kick your shoe and look away askance.
You're totally alone.
He's quite completely gone.

This is surely why, through time, each culture and each creed
When faced with Death's finality has felt an urgent need
To create a grand Hereafter, an Eternal Paradise.
Where loved ones wait to greet us. It all sounds very nice.
But is it really true?
You don't know, do you?

But, meantime, for us mortals left here, wond'ring, on the ground
The only thing you really know is that he won't be around.
You can forget the funfair gypsy with a tea towel round her head:
The 'quick' will never hear again from their beloved 'dead'.
You're by yourself.
He's somewhere else!

He won't be there to argue with or p'raps, sometimes, agree
When an issue of great moment needs resolving urgently.
Like: who was the greatest trumpet player that Basie ever had?
Was it Edison or Clayton or, p'raps just maybe, Thad?
Giving Eddie Calvert's name
Will never get a laugh again!

Your mind runs back to the funeral parlour when you stood with trembling lip.
Saying: 'Ta ta y'old bastard. Safe journey on your trip!'
Then, with arm round his widow's shoulder, what else was there to say?
Only what a zillion others have said on such a day:
'Deep down in my heart I know
We'll meet again somewhere.'

'High above the chimney tops
Where troubles melt like lemon drops …!'

***

I wrote this in September 1976 at the end of that year's glorious summer. The erstwhile constant companion for whom it was written hardly spoke to me again after I gave it to her. Ah well, that's a poet's lot!

As Autumn Falls

What use to say, as Autumn falls:
'I should have loved you then!'

You didn't appear in the springtime,
Though you certainly were there,
Planted deep like a seedling,
Feeding calmly whilst, unaware,
I desperately clung to an old dream
That left me no thoughts to spare.

It was suddenly in the summer
That I first began to find
You were a new dream waking,
Taking shape, because my mind
Unwittingly had nurtured you
To arrive at this perfect time.

Unnoticed and quite naturally
I realised we'd become
Unconsciously companions
Within a crowd that some
Might call, at the best, incongruous
To take excitement from.

All vaguely 'misplaced' people
With nothing better to do:
One endearingly shy youth;
Another less so, who
Was keen to recruit for his own 'scene',
(Though I think it excluded you!)

I should have pulled you away to Putney,
Sucking your mouth as we fled;
Thrown you down like a chattel
Upon that enormous bed;
Wriggled you out of your long dress
And bitten your flesh 'til it bled.

But, instead, I allowed us to linger
In that crowd where it couldn't occur.
Studying you in silence
And wondering who you were.
Still longing for my old dream,
Comparing you to her.

*

But what an exceptional summer!
And how brown your body turned!
As we sat outside in our lunch breaks
Drinking wine whilst the high sun burned.

*

Then I feared for my lack of decision
Which had left you still unclaimed.
For I sensed a shadow of menace come,
Unmentioned and unnamed,
With a style whose boldness made it clear
He was playing a different game.

So I called for you to come to me.
You giggled down the phone.
Said you would ring me later;
Made me wait, irate, alone
And, suffering in that scorching sun,
I realised I'd never known

Just what motives moved you:
What dreams you were searching for.
Weeks watching you and wondering
Had in no way made me sure
Whether you were warm and sensitive
Or a cold, self-centred whore.

*

But how the summer became you!
It really made you glow!
And, as long as you laughed and inspired me,
What more did I need to know?

*

But mysteries and secrets
Will consume us so!
Forcing us to ask things
That we're not supposed to know!

The summer had seemed to be endless
But it's vanishing at last
And what was the wonderful present
Has become the perfect past.

The summer was our season!
I've let it slip away!
Reading too many secrets
Into things you didn't say.

It's strange how little's happened:
My old dream hasn't died!
You're like two different sisters
Existing side by side.
Neither really chosen
And neither one denied.

But time has overtaken us;
The wind is bringing rain.
That sun which so delighted us
Won't shine as bright again.
What use to say, as autumn falls:
'I should have loved you then!'

***

1979 and another tale of unrequited romance.

A Drink Before Christmas

A chance for me to sit and gaze
Adoringly at you.

Knightsbridge in December
Was a pleasure to behold.
The windows of the bijoux shops
Were spangled red and gold.

But so many people crowded us
And the wind was bitter cold.
You took my hand for comfort
And the gesture warmed my soul.

I'd hoped that you might spare some time
From the busy life you led
To share with me a Christmas drink.
Though we'd never shared a bed.

Just a drink, a laugh, a chat,
And, perhaps, a kiss: adieu.
A chance for me to sit and gaze
Adoringly at you.

I led you across the busy road
Hoping to find again
One of the quaint, old London pubs
I used to drink in way back when.
And then:

*

By chance, a turning brought the sound
Of brassy carolling and we found,
Outside a pub, had taken stand
A small, dishevelled oompah band.

As we approached, they marched inside
And, with the swing doors opened wide,
We felt invited to take part
And join the show about to start.

And, all at once, it was Christmas time,
The climax of the year.
As if a star
Above the bar
Had led us to it here.

Surrounded by brass harmony
We sat beside a Christmas tree
Whilst hymns we'd known since we were young
Were re-remembered and re-sung.

It raised the conflict of our role:
The Pagan flesh and the Christian soul.
To praise this child we called divine
While drinking Guinness and white wine.

Then, suddenly, a quiet came.
The oompah band was gone.
Of what they'd played
An echo stayed.

But we were quite alone.
Then memories of Christmas Past,
Of old affairs that didn't last
Returned like carols to your mind
Glad they'd not been left behind.

'How complicated life can be,'
You sighed and I smiled wistfully.
Regretting that I never knew
The carefree girl that once was you.

But, all too soon, came closing time.
The final bell had gone.
We were in retreat
To an empty street
And, soon, I would sleep alone.

Yet, come another Christmas time,
I'll have a memory
Of a longed-for gift
That I ached to lift
From beside a tinselled tree.

* * *

1986 Given to a long term girl friend on her leaving for California to take up with some guy she'd met on holiday. Her response: a girlish laugh and: 'Oh, don't be ridiculous!' (She didn't stay away long and we're still great mates.)

Crushed Love

A spirit in a tomb

Love, like a flower, will wilt and fade
If left to run its time.
For nothing in this life can stay
Indefinitely sublime.

And yet, a flower, if plucked while live,
And pressed to early death
Will keep its springtime colour bright
As when it once had breath.

So, if a flower that's killed while young
Retains its petals' bloom
Then crushed love, too, might cheat its death:
A spirit in a tomb.

***

For one of my sisters on her seventieth birthday

For Pam

gazing skyward you want to shout....... !

Seventy years old
And what do you know
That you weren't well aware of long, long ago?
What new wisdom
Have you gleaned
Since you were,
Let's say, seventeen?

Is the old lady
That now is you
Wiser than the ingénue
Who set out bravely
To pursue
A life that then seemed
Utterly new?

And what adventures did you find
To beat the adventures that your mind
Had eagerly dreamed about and planned
Long before 'Real Life' began?

Instinctively your mind had sensed
Far more than you've learned from experience.
Life has only proved to you
What your young self already knew.

That our existence here must be
A constant, baffling mystery.
And, gazing skyward, you want to shout:
'What the fuck is this about?'

*A reappraisal of the legacy of Victor Silvester
and the strict tempo dance:*

The Joy Of Ballroom Dancing

*You hum again each lovely tune
Remembering how you 'Wished on the Moon.'*

Maybe it's not too late for me yet
But missing the chance to learn how to dance
Is something I deeply regret.
How foolish was the sneering youth
Who couldn't recognise the truth:
That dancing with steps is a social grace
That no other skill can quite replace.

Yes, I used to jig around
And picked up some praise in my younger days
But there came a time when I found,
At wedding receptions or formal balls,
Men of my age came across as crass fools
When they got up and tried to do the Twist
While kids in the crowd were jerking a wrist.

But if I glance towards the stand
And find that they've hired a smartly attired
Old fashioned strict tempo band
I know that some 'old folk' will show
Just how to dance the 'quick, quick, slow'
And even the kids you'd expect to guffaw
Will watch the display with something like awe.

No clenched fists punching the air.
No gyrating hips, no puckered up lips.
The movement is so debonair.
Gliding like swans round the floor
Demonstrating true Terpsichore.
How perfectly adult and civilised
Is this entertainment I'd once despised.

And just occasionally, still,
An old vinyl record will start, say: 'Dancing on my Heart'
And you can sense a certain thrill
As Poggy Pogson's saxophone
With its mellifluous, warm tone,
Prompts a number of elderly pairs
To ease themselves up from their wooden chairs.

Clearly enjoying the chance
To hum or to croon along with the tune
As they take to the floor for a dance.
Then gracefully they'll glide,
Swaying with each practised stride.
Old ladies become their young selves again
Coy in the arms of their portly old men.

And I s'pose that that's the root of its charms.
Like modest foreplay as two warm bodies sway
In the loose grip of each other's arms.
A chance to get to know and vet
The stranger you have lately met.
While sweet music wafts in the air above
And coaxes you both to fall in love.

No screeching above the 'House Sound'
No cupping your ear in order to hear
The name of the partner you've found.
You'll clearly hear her every word.
Each 'Whisper in the Dark' is heard.
No other dancers in the crowd
Are being forced to talk too loud.

So, 'While a Cigarette Is Burning'
And you catch a girl's glance suggesting a chance
That a deeply felt yearning
For the thrill of Romance
Has arrived 'Out of Nowhere'.
Will your 'Foolish Heart' dare?
To ask for a dance.

Then who knows but maybe
As your two bodies sway, she'll be happy to stay
'Till', eventually,
To the band's closing tune,
Their songstress will croon:
'Who's Taking You Home Tonight?'
And you ask if you might.

Not for a quick 'bit of tail'!
A hot shag in the car and then both say: 'Ta, Tar.'
No, that's just not true 'Ballroom' style.
A lingering kiss at her front door.
A promise that you will see her some more.
Then, it's back to your separate beds
Where melodies will spin around in your heads.

The hypnotic cadence of the dance
The warm, sweet vibrato of Senior Oscar Grasso
Has put your poor mind in a trance.
You hum again each lovely tune
Rememb'ring how you 'Wished on the Moon'
That someone might step '… Out of a Dream'.
And take you to 'Heav'n on a Moonbeam'!

'Long Ago and Faraway'
You wished for just this: a look, a kiss.
Now, p'raps, 'Love's Here to Stay'.
But then, what if it suddenly ends
With one of you saying let's be 'Just Friends'.
You pray that one 'Lovely Weekend'
Your new partner says: "How 'bout it then?

'Be My Life's Companion', please.
Be Jack and Jill in our home on a hill
And there make our own memories."
You try to sleep in vain
And, yet, there's ecstasy in pain.
You're somewhere 'Between a Kiss and a Sigh.'
You just can't sleep, it's useless to try.

That entrancing, strict tempo is set.
Tunes spin round your head from above your warm bed.
Those melodies will linger yet.
All night long you will find your heart go
In time to the pulsing: quick, quick, slow!
That 'Kiss To Build a Dream On' you shared
Has left your poor 'Heart and Soul' bared.

As you toss and you turn trying to sleep.
'It Can't Be Wrong!' you repeat all night long.
Your blankets roll up in a heap.
You find you've become 'A Prisoner Of Love'
Her smile is all that you can think of.
As you lie there with both eyes shut tight
Saying: 'Stars Fell On *The Locarno* Last Night.'

And all through the next waking week
You will anticipate the first arranged date
When you might find the soul mate you seek.
Will the stars twinkle and shine
That evening, 'About a Quarter To Nine!'?
''Til Then', your heart's a 'Dancing Thing'
That, all day long, just wants to sing.

Will there be 'Hands Across The Table'
And sweet words to say in a corner café?
Or will you both feel unable
To build a fresh enchantment from
That lovely evening now it's gone?

Is there just the slightest chance
You will realise at a glance:
It was just the music of the dance?

***

The Daffodil Patch

For just how long have they been here?
Who planted them and in what year?

Unfailingly each passing year
Our yellow daffodils appear.
Uncoaxed, untended, ignored, unfed
From a patch of garden that had seemed quite dead.
Suddenly we realise
That, before our winter-weary eyes,
New life has risen; hope has sprung
And a re-awakening has begun.

The lingering trace of Autumn's gold
Stays a while, though the breeze turns cold.
But then the garden, week on week,
Becomes a dark place, cold and bleak.
Where icy squalls of wind-lashed rain
Chastise us with a whip-like pain.
But, sight of this bright-petalled pool
Makes the landscape seem less cruel.

For just how long have they been here?
Who planted them and in what year?
I know from the deeds of our property
That the building is nineteenth century.
But no official mention is made
Of the plants and shrubs that had then been laid.
So I stand here foolishly
Wondering what they've seen of history.

Did a family, long ago
Awaiting news from Flanders, ('where the poppies blow'),
Take solace from these lovely flowers
To ease them through their anxious hours?
And how many sick men have stood right here
Knowing it was their final year
To gaze upon each petalled head
Because, by autumn, they'd be dead?

Yes, mortal creatures come and go
Their time is finite here below.
Within their own allotted span
They live and die as best they can.
But at the start of each new year
These daffodils will reappear
To lift the spirit, cheer the soul.
A lovely vision to behold!

Oh no! Here comes that ginger cat!
'Clear off, Scabby! Scat, boy! Scat!'

***

Hold That Door!

I'll always hold ajar the door
For anybody, rich or poor,

It isn't old world 'chivalry'
To display the common courtesy
Of holding a door when passing through
So that the person following you,
Or approaching from the other side
Will find the door still open wide
And needn't falter in their stride.

There's no pretence of 'gallant knight'
To simply do what is polite.
And those for whom you've stepped aside
Have no need to feel patronised.
I'll always hold ajar the door
For anybody, rich or poor,
As a gesture, nothing more.

But it's becoming commonplace
To find a door slammed in your face.
Or some oaf will just barge past
As you stand holding the swing door fast.
And how often is it true
That someone you have ushered through
Doesn't even acknowledge you.

And then, of course, increasingly
There are ladies who will seem to be
Convinced that your polite display
Is demeaning them in some strange way.
Making them feel second class
As if you'd whistled as they passed.
Or winked and tried to feel their arse.

This quite annoys me, I admit,
But I find it helps a little bit
To shout: 'You fucking ignorant piece of shit!'

**

Yes, I used to watch the old Rin Tin Tin movies at the Saturday morning pictures.

Woof, Woof

I don't really 'do' dogs

I've always struggled to understand
How so many normal people can
Take on a dog quite happily
And treat it as one of the family.

The creatures bark and scratch and whine;
Demand attention all the time.
They take over totally
All sense of domestic harmony.

'Oh no, you can't sit there!
You know that's Fido's favourite chair!'
'Well stuff that dog' you might exclaim.
But it seems that it's given prior claim.

They snort and snuffle. Yelp and smell.
And what they're thinking, who can tell?
And this is what I find the worst
In all dog owners: they are cursed

With a feeling that they have a way
Of knowing what dogs are trying to say.
'Oh. Bless him,' they exclaim
When the dog grunts at a TV game.

'He really likes the interplay
When that cheeky MC has his say.'
'What?' you feel compelled to shout.
But you let it ride; yet there's no doubt

That people you used to know as friends;
As perfectly likeable citizens.
Have, somewhere along the way,
Picked up a problem. You're dismayed,

To find that rational, reas'nable folk.
Folk who once enjoyed a joke.
Have developed issues of mental health.
Madness has crept on them by stealth.

You find them on their hands and knees
Saying things like: 'Pretty please,'
Or: 'Itchy koo', or 'Mwuh, mwuh, mwuh,'
While tickling the chin of their wretched cur.

Insanity! Don't you agree?
It will never, ever happen to me!

*

'Hallo, Mart What's up?
A favour? Anytime! How much?
Mind you, I haven't had that fiver back from the other night.
But, well, alright.

Hospital! Oh dear.
Sounds a bit nasty. I'm sorry to hear.
And how's your mother? She coping okay?
Sorry again. What more can I say?

So you're going up there. And Jan, too.
Well, that's what sons are supposed to do.
You're stepping in. Good for you!
So what's the favour? What can I do?

Charlie!—Well—tut, tut, tut
I don't really "do" dogs—but.
And he's built like a donkey. A sizeable mutt!
But—yeah. Of course. I'll be happy to, mate.

Pity that Yvonne's away.
'Cos she'd just love the chance to— play.
But she's in Dublin for a day or two.
So bring the pooch round and tell me what to do.

Does he have a kennel and a bone?
Other things he thinks are his own.
He sleeps on the sofa—well I s'pose I could—
Oh, he's got his own blanket. Well, that'll be good.

And what does he eat? Lightly-seasoned road kill?
Oh, you'll bring some special stuff round. But still —
He'll probably want some table scraps.
Chunks of red meat or something like that.

Quorn and tofu! And some occasional chicken stew.
Well, I'll leave it up to you.
Yeah. Come round soon as you like.
I'm staying in all night.'

        *

'I don't really "do" dogs,' I was muttering still
When the doorbell rang and I felt a chill.
'This is really good of you, mate,'
Mart said forcibly. 'And sorry it's so late.'

'No prob,' I said affably. 'I'm never in bed 'fore midnight.
And how's your dad doing? Alright?'
'Oh yeah, He's fine. But mum's upset.
Something like this always makes her fret.'

''Course,' I said. 'Yer old man's knockin' on a bit.
Not a good age to take a hit.'
'Ohhh—he sometimes likes to put it on.
But, as you say: he's not that young.'

'Now you know Charlie, don't you. Met him lots before.'
'Yes,' I said, shifting uneasily at the door.
The beast was even bigger than I remembered. Not much smaller than a cow.
'Now say hello, Charlie. You know exactly how.'

And, obediently, the dog held out a paw and said: 'Woof, woof.'
The paw in my hand was more like a hoof.
But I smiled as I said: 'Good evening, Charlie. How d'you do?'
'Wuff, wuff,' he answered. 'Oh, he's already taken to you,'

Jan told me happily. 'It couldn't start out much better.'
'Well, he certainly seems a well-mannered critter.
Never mind house-trained. He seems to know his social stuff.'
And I found myself bending to stroke the thing. 'Wuff.'

I was surprised when it actually licked my hand.
'Oh, yes. He really likes you,' enthused Jan.
For myself, I felt slightly alarmed.
Felt I'd like a warm tap to rinse my palm.

But at least it hadn't given me a bite.
It seemed that we might get along all right.
'Well come on in,' I said. 'Have a drink before you go.'
'No, that's very kind,' said Mart. 'But we've gotta get moving with the show.'

'Brenda's waiting up 'til we arrive,' said Jan.
'And it's a bit of a journey in the van.'
The 'van', a BMW four-door convertible was parked outside.
'Are you sure the elastic bands will be up to the ride?'

I enquired concernedly.
'Mart always carries spares,' laughed she.
It was then that I noticed an enormous sack
That Jan was holding at her back.

'We've brought a few of Charlie's things,' she said.
'Some food and the blanket to put on his bed.
And we should've given you this to begin,'
Mart said, holding out a magnum of gin

'Oh, no need for something like that, mate.'
'Well—we thought you might appreciate—!
Oh, and here's something else you might need!'
He handed me a strong, brown, leather lead.

And a moment later they were gone
Leaving me absolutely all alone.
'Wuff, wuff.' Well, not totally on my own.
I found myself with this furry, overgrown—

Hand-licking, woofing son of a horse.
I could think of nothing that could be worse.
'Wuff, wuff,' said the creature looking up at me.
And it seemed to be giving me sympathy.

*

Mart told me that they'd fed the thing
And Jan said I'd find everything
That the dog might need to eat
Portioned out in bags; with the odd little treat.

'So, Chazz,' I murmured, 'it's just you and me,'
'Wuff,' said the dog consolingly.
'What're the sort of things you go for?'
And the dog jumped up on our leather sofa.

Which rolled slightly backwards under its weight.
'Hang on a minute, Chazz. Just wait.
Let's look in this enormous sack
For the blanket "mummy" said she'd packed.'

'Wuff,' said the beast and, obediently,
Slipped down from the sofa and came over to me
To watch as I searched in his goodies sack,
Taking out items and putting them back.

I held up a rubber bone that I found;
But it let me drop it on the ground.
Then it stuck its enormous snout
Into the sack as if to sort out

Some favourite toys that might be there.
It pulled out a ragged teddy bear
Completely devoid of any hair
And, seemingly, nibbled everywhere.

'Oh, looks as if you like old Teddy.
Well: Steady, Teddy. Let's get ready!'
'Woof, woof, woof,' came a gentle bark.
And its tail rotated in an arc.

I found its woollen blanket and laid the huge sack down
But it rolled it around as it lay on the ground
Then its outsized nose, damp as peeled cucumber
Nudged at my hand as if guiding it under

The parcels of food and the odd doggy toy
It seemed to want something: 'What is it, boy?'
It dug with its nose to the sack's very bottom
And pulled out a pillow wrapped in red cotton;

'Wruff!' it exclaimed and poked with its chin
To show that the thing bore a picture of him.
'So, you've brought your own personal pillow case, then?'
I said and it 'wuff-wuffed' again.

'Well then, Chazz, you've got all that you need!'
And it gave one more 'wuff' to show it agreed.
'"Mummy" told me you've already been fed.
So, I think it's time now that you were in bed!'

Glancing at the sofa and the size of the beast
It seemed it could use two feet more at the least.
But when I spread the blanket down
It hopped up and curled itself around

So that it was sitting upright and alert;
And I sensed it felt just a little bit hurt
At being sent to its 'beddy baws' when
It was barely even a quarter to ten.

It was staring at the TV screen,
Blank and dark as it had always been
Since my wife took off for Dublin town
And left me mooching around on my own.

But I almost sensed that Chazz was saying:
'What's on the box? Let's get it playing.'
So I found the remote and duly aimed it
At the pitch black screen until a frame lit.

Presenting the usual nonentities
Of giggling media celebrities.
Even the dog seemed unimpressed
By the plastic personae, improperly dressed.

So I pressed a few buttons until I found
A 'nature' programme with sheep running round.
Chazz seemed to like the sights that it saw
Never mind tofu: this was 'food' in the raw.

So I left it to savour its own fantasy
And turned my attention to what lifted me,
Recently I'd found, I have to say,
That my limbs weren't over-exerted, per se.

I no longer smashed those little black balls
Against a squash court's waiting blank walls
So my blood circulation was, let's say
A little less 'fluid' than yesterday.

But I'd found a solution, a real substitute
And it didn't require a flannel track suit:
I'd downloaded some tracks on my mobile phone
To jig round to at night while on my own.

When Yvonne said: 'Goodnight' and retired to her bed
I'd slap some large headphones over my head
Turn down the lights so that no one could see
Then: 'Vout-a-Roonie. Ooh Ow A-woowee!'

I slipped off my slip-ons and felt for my phone.
Plugged in the cans and was set to get going.
Just had to check that the curtains were drawn
Before I began the jigging around.

To get the ball rolling, I pressed on a track
That never failed to send chills down my back:
Wynonie 'Blues' Harris with the Millender band.
And big Bull Moose Jackson lending a hand.

'Oh Babe!' he's about to say.
Okay fellas: take it away.
And I 'wiggled' and I 'squiggled' as the reed section riffed.
While the dog on the sofa gave an uneasy shift.

Of course, Chazz couldn't hear what was on the headphones
It thought it was there with a madman, alone
As I skipped and I flipped and joined in out loud
Until Bull Moose's tenor slid out of the crowd.

Then something like pure dementia set in
The dog on the sofa jumped out of its skin.
I used to be a bit of a limbo 'star'
Making a prat of myself under the bar.

So as Bull Moose honked his tenor sax
I bent right over on my back
So that I felt the circulation flow
As I tested just how low I could go,

The answer, of course, was: 'not very'
And, soon, I came over all 'unnecessary'!
But the dog saved me from doing much harm
When I felt that great snout nudging my arm.

I picked myself up from the floor
And was helped to my feet by an enormous paw.
When I looked at the beast I saw
That it had the remote clasped in its jaw.

It seemed it was bored with the 'nature' show.
'Could I change channels?' it wanted to know.
Or, at least that's what I inferred
From the general stance of the oversized cur.

The truth is, I hadn't a clue
On how to change channels. What should I do
To switch the settings, find something new?
Something this dog would take liking to?

But Chazz took total control.
Put the remote on the floor and dabbed with its paw
Until it seemed to like a programme it saw:
A cookery contest with raw meat galore.

'I don't think Mart feeds you right!'
I ventured to say and got a slight
'Wruff' as if in agreement.
And I knew just what it meant.

'Tofu!' I murmured. 'That's not what you need.
I think you crave a healthier feed!'
And I was sure that Charlie agreed:
'Wuff, wuff!' it confided, looking at me.

'Well, sorry, Chazz, but I've got my instructions
And changing your diet just might cause some ructions.'
But the dog was distracted and seemed not to hear
Salivating at raw beef on the TV.

So the two of us sat and watched a disparate crew
Who'd been tasked with preparing a Moroccan-based stew.
The dog leaned right onto the edge of its seat
At the sight of all that well-seasoned meat.

'Yum, yum,' I said as the stew was stirred.
And 'Wuff, wuff, wuff!' the dog demurred.
Then, after a while I was a little alarmed
To find the dog ease its head onto my arm.

'This is cosy, Chazz, isn't it?' I said
And I could swear that it nodded its enormous head.
At least an hour slipped past in this way
Until three of the chefs were voted away.

Then, sensing that Chazz had had enough
I said: 'Bedtime?' And it said: 'Wuff.'
I was a little concerned that the huge beast just might
Want to share my bed for the night.

The way it'd been cosying up had, in truth,
Reminded me of girls I'd met in my youth
Who seemed overkeen to move up a notch.
A situation that I'd learned to watch.

But, no! I'd misread the signs.
The dog was happy with its bed, not mine.
With just that well-chewed teddy pressed to its head.
So I said : 'Night, night, Charlie,' and headed for bed.

*

Next day was Saturday and usually
Yvonne brings me a warm cup of tea
And tells me it's late: a quarter to three!
She thinks she's so funny. 'Oh, tee bloody hee.'

But today I thought it expected of me
To get up at dawn and just check to see
That the donkey on the sofa had had a good night's sleep
So I eased downstairs in jim jams to take a quick peep.

I found it in the kitchen curled up beside the fridge
Waiting for its breakfast of tofu or something which
Might help to start a dog's day
And put the appetite at bay.

'So, what d'you fancy, Chazz?' I said.
'Some rashers of bacon and a slice of fried bread?'
And, though it wagged its tail, I felt it wouldn't be quite right
To disregard the guidelines Mart had given me last night.

So I looked out a pack of Jan's well-seasoned quorn
And put it in a brown bowl with a doggy picture on.
'Wruff!' was Chazz' reaction as it started tucking in.
Nudging at the dish with its Desperate Dan sized chin.

I lied a little bit when I said 'the crack of dawn'.
By the time I'd finished breakfast it was more like late-mid-morn.
And Chazz was looking restless. I knew a dog that size
Needed lots and lots of outdoor exercise.

So, intent on doing my duty,
I got myself suited out and booted
For a 'walkies' round the local park.
When the dog saw its lead it gave a bark.

'Steady boy,' I murmured like a farmer in his field
And Charlie, bless him, settled down and 'heeled'.
Then it was out of the door and: forward! An old man and his dog.
Let's pray it doesn't run away so help me please, sweet God!

I was a little surprised when, out in the street,
All of the many people we'd meet
Would stop and bend to stroke the pooch
Saying things like: 'Awwww, coochie cooch!'

I just stood and smiled as they cooed.
I didn't want to seem unduly rude.
They obviously thought that the dog was mine
And I was quite happy to go along with that line.

The dog seemed to love the attention it got.
To be tickled and stroked and why would it not?
Although, I have to say if it happened to me
I'm not sure just how delighted I'd be

To have total strangers down on their knees
Hands on my body. I might just say: 'Please,
Have a care. Take your hands off my hips
And why on earth are you puckering your lips?'

But the dog's response was 'wuff' and then 'wuff'.
It could quite clearly not get enough
Of the overt affection on display.
I suppose that dogs are just made that way.

But, eventually I'd have to say,
'Well, best be off then. Have a nice day.'
And head for the gates of our local park.
Two gambolling funsters out for a lark.

*

The ornate ironwork of the park's main gates
Were open wide with bolts in place,
Inviting people passing by
To take a breath and come inside.
And what a wonderland awaited
Those who entered. So elated
Would they be
At the vision they would see.

Rolling grassland with wooded copses
Beset with squirrels and occasional foxes.
And such a musky, perfumed waft
Of early autumn: moist and soft.
To breathe the air excited me
And all around me I could see
The summer leaves that once were green
Now turning sepia; quite serene

Was this vast and verdant public space
Maintained that citizens might embrace
A sense of the wonder we'd been given
By mother nature or some God in heaven.
But it didn't really matter what moved
The councillors who ultimately approved
The expenditure required to keep it intact
I was happy to pay through my council tax.

The dog was tugging at its leash.
And I thanked it for giving my life new lease.
'This is alright, Chazz, is it not?'
I said, kneeling down in an awkward squat
To release the strap and free the beast.
Which immediately took off to feast
On the lovely treats that this arena
Offered us. My lungs felt cleaner

As they sucked at the gentle breeze, delighted
To be filled with a fragrant scent, unblighted
By the toxic poison of the air
That surrounded us elsewhere.

Dwelling on these idle musings,
I realised I was losing
Sight of the oversized, barking pet
That was in my charge. To neglect

It here would be foolish of me
I couldn't take the chance that it might run free.
The two finger whistle has never quite been
A talent I've nurtured. Know what I mean.

And I couldn't bring myself to shout:
'Oi, Charlie! Come on out!'
So I was quite relieved when I spotted the dog
Dipping its nose in what looked like a bog.

Edging t'ward it I could make out
It was more like a pond that was tempting its snout.
'Come on now, Charlie. Let's find you a stick
To run around after. That'll do the trick.'

But, as I came nearer, he pulled from the bog
What looked to me like a soaking wet log.
Then, securing the thing in its teeth on the ground
He picked the 'stick' up and shook it around.

He'd found a toy his size to play with
For me to toss and him run away with.
'Oh, okay then, Charlie, This'll be good:
You want me to throw you this wet, rotten wood!'

And, picking it up with one struggling hand,
I heaved the log forward and watched it land
No more than three feet away
And then, to my dismay,

Splinters of rotten, wet wood pieces sprawled
And, from the log's interior, slugs and beetles crawled.
'Ok, Chazz,' I whispered, feeling slightly sick
'Let's try and find you a smaller, drier stick.'

'Wuff. Wuff!'

*

Finding a better stick wasn't hard with all the surrounding trees.
I soon came on a broken branch that I could toss with ease.
Charlie was delighted. He barked and wagged his tail.
We were on the grassland but still I couldn't fail

To spot the people stopping on the path
To watch the dog. They smiled and laughed.
And there suddenly came back to me something I've always heard:
'Get yourself a dog if you wanna pull a bird!'

I'd never put this to the test
But folk who thought that they knew best
Were absolutely adamant
That was all you'd really need or want.

If you couldn't afford a flashy car
You should get yourself a Labrador.
Or an elk hound or a husky or—
You were sure to meet women by the score.

And, even as I mulled this thought
I picked up Chazz's stick and caught
The almost mystic, spectral sight
Of a vision of delight.

Out with her own dog but taking time
To bend and tickle Chazz. Who was mine.
I quickened my step because it seemed that she
Was waiting there to speak to me.

'What an enormous dog,' she said,
Bending down to scratch its head.
'Wuff, wuff, wuff,' Chazz said to me,
Wagging its tail excitedly.

'Yes,' I said. 'I'm going to buy it a saddle so
That I can charge for a ride. Fiver a go!'
I was delighted that she laughed at this
But then looked at me, slightly amiss:

'You can't call him "it",' she said scoldingly.
'You've surely got to call him "he".
'Oh well: "He",' I said obediently
(And made a note for the future mentally).

'But what on earth does he eat?' she then asked curiously.
And I was glad to find she was talking to me
And not the dog as I'd found was the case
With others who'd stopped for a doggy embrace.

'Would you believe that tofu and quorn
Is all the overgrown mutt lives on.'
It warmed me to see her laugh loudly at this.
I couldn't have felt better if she'd given me a kiss.

'Oh, Pliny likes red meat,' she told me
And I raised my eyebrows at the name 'Pliny'
'"Fortune favours the bold!"' I said grandly
Looking at the little, black pooch by her knee.

She seemed quite impressed with this quotation
And said 'Oh, that's a perfect translation.
You did Latin at school, did you?'
'Well,' I said. 'I sat in class but never knew

Just what was going on: ablative absolutes and the rest.
I couldn't nowadays pass a test.
I was okay with "Amo, amas, amat",
But really got no further than that.'

She looked at me in sympathy, saying:
'Ohh, you should have stuck with it. Maybe
You'd have found a wealth of thought
Valid then and still being taught.'

'Really?' I replied, lamely as I examined her anew.
'It seems to mean a lot to you.'.
'Well—yes,' she told me, hesitantly,
'I'm off to uni tomorrow you see.

To study the Greats of History'
'"The 'Greats'", I responded. 'Who would they be?
The Sporting Icons like Mohamed Ali?
Or Bobby Moore and just maybe

Martina Navratilova and the things that she …?'
'Be serious,' she scolded immediately.
And I was glad to find
That she didn't seem to mind

Me 'playing the fool' as I so often did.
To disguise a deep ignorance that I liked to keep hid.
'No! The GREATS!' she protested laughing at me.
'The minds that have altered our history!'

'The "Literae Humanitories"
Whose "tomes", even now, are spread out before us.'
'Well, good for them,' I said with no hesitation.
'Yes, their thoughts underpin civilisation!'

She was laughing at me as she proclaimed vibrantly.
Some of the wisdom that had quite escaped me.
'And they all spoke Latin?' I suggested.
And there was a withering look as she protested:

'Latin, German and some Russian, too.'
'And you speak all these languages, too, do you?'
She was still laughing I have to say.
My stupid chit chat hadn't spoiled the day.

'And what moved you to pursue the Latin tongue?
It seems to have lost its appeal to the young-
-er generation.' I asked curiously.
'Surely 'media manipulations' would be

A 'trendier' pursuit. Or some other nonsense that,
Today, makes up the educational twat
That the next generation is being fed upon.
The idea of 'knowledge' being long gone.'

She gave me a look of sad disdain.
But she knew that I was kidding, again!
'I'm going to be a lawyer!' She proclaimed.
'So, a bit of Latin does no harm.

And, I have to say, once I'd started studying,
My teacher at school, – not that young,
Made me realise the wealth of wisdom,
The absolutely perfect vision,

Of our ancestors, long ago.
A different age and culture but, you know:
I found it to be, for what it's worth,
An understanding of life on Earth.'

'So, does that explain "Pliny" as a name for your pet?'
I asked. 'Why not Rover, Barker or Brett?'
This lovely girl leaned close to me, whispering confidentially:
'No! Pliny, as a puppy used to bark a lot, you see

And Gramps complained 'til his dying day
That the dog had an awful lot to say.
So, to keep him happy, I proclaimed
That "Pliny" had to be his name

'Because Pliny, God help us, in his day
Had more than enough that he wanted to say.'
'And did your grandpa speak Latin?' I enquired
And she leaned a bit closer as if inspired

To tell me earnestly: 'No, Gramps, (my GREAT grandad),
Came over on a boat from Trinidad
To drive a London Transport omnibus.'
'Well,' I ventured, 'lucky for us.

'Cos the London bus, running reliably
"Underpins civilisation", for me.'
Smiling witheringly she continued that he
Eventually earned an engineering degree

That secured him a place on the team at Fords
Where he won a lot of industry awards.
I looked at her with unmasked amazement:
'Well, you come from a line of high achievement!'

She shrugged, saying: 'We're not shirkers.
Just a bunch of quite hard workers!'
'And you're off to uni tomorrow. Where?'
'Balliol, Oxford!' she told me and stared

Into space with a smile on her face.
'That's a bit special,' I told her, impressed
And her smile was filled with youth's bright flame.
As if she were dreaming of fortune and fame.

'Well, really good luck,' I sincerely said,
'And don't let the "drug culture" mess up your head.'
I felt this was something I had to say.
To guide this ingenue safe on her way,

As if she were a grand-daughter of mine.
I was pleased when she said: 'No, I'll stick with red wine.'
Then with just a soft touch on my arm
She was off with her small dog to keep her from harm.

I watched her as she skipped away.
Her life before her, as they say.
And Charlie the dog looked up at me
'He' seemed to be smiling happily.

As if saying: 'Just look at who
I can introduce you to!'

*

Yes, it was clear that having Chazz at my side
Was going to make me lots of new friends. And I spied
The next likely candidate: a not unattractive older lady
Approaching with her dog and smiling gaily,

Lips already puckered up in readiness
For the compulsory doggie caress.
'Oh, what an enormous creature,' she said to me
Settling herself down on one knee.

'What on earth do you feed him. Must say
A pound and a half of red meat every day
Wouldn't go far with a critter this size.
And, oh what lovely, adorable eyes.'

I had an uneasy feeling the 'adorable eyes'
Wasn't the main attraction, or the dog's enormous size.
And it was not long before she was revealing
A lot more of how she was feeling.

'Dogs are such good company,' she sighed
Straightening up to stand by my side.
'Since my divorce, young Rupert here,'
She gestured to her dog who was scuffling near,

'Has been my one companion. My little pride and joy.
Come here, Rupert. Give me a kiss. Good boy.'
She knelt down again to waggle Rupert's ears
And something in the way she moved aroused my worst fears.

Though feeling slightly flattered by this overt carry on
I felt she should know I was a happily married man.
'Yes,' I said. 'My wife loves dogs. In fact she
Is even fonder of our Charlie here than me.'

Rupert's 'mum' took this news stoically.
And Charlie's tail wagged as he looked up at me.
So I patted his back, tickled his neck and then
Threw another stick to send

Him racing off which gave me the welcome chance
To say 'good day' to Rupert's mum and advance
Along the path until another lady accosted me.
Perhaps I was being a little unfair and it was only vanity

That convinced me I was somehow an object of desire
But this next lady with a dog seemed to be on fire.
She told me that her name was Fay
And had recently become a divorcée.

Gently fondling her behind and wriggling all the while
She told me life was so lonely that she found it hard to smile.
But Charlie, out there, prowling, running around,
Rushed back to me and I sensed the dog had found

Something urgent taking place not far away.
So, making my excuses, I said goodbye to Fay
And followed Charlie onto the grass
To find out why he was making such a fuss.

Then a sad looking couple came into sight:
An elderly man who couldn't stand upright
Pushing a wheelchair while clutching a stick
And the wheelchair's occupant looked really sick.

The blank look of dementia was there on her face.
Mouth wide open as she stared into space.
It was a tragic sight to behold, I agree
But I couldn't understand why Charlie was showing it to me.

The dog nudged me nearer and, reluctantly
I followed his lead acting nonchalantly.
Then the hunchbacked old man shaded his eyes,
Straightened himself slightly and, to my surprise,

Said: 'Fishmongers Arms, about sixty-three!'
'That would've been me,' I had to agree.
And, suddenly, the mists of memory cleared.
A vision of their younger selves appeared:

It was Micky and Madge the skip jiving pair
Whose expertise had been beyond compare.
A circle would form when they went to town.
Punters would cheer as he swung her around.

Over his shoulder then down on the floor.
Whatever they did, the crowd yelled for more.
'You remember Madge, don't you?' he said.
Casting a sad eye and whisp'ring: 'Out of her head!'

He didn't need to point this out: it was abundantly clear
That Alzheimer's meant she was no longer here.
'Hey diddle, diddle. Hey diddle, diddle,' she was repeating.
'Bloody demented,' he whispered. 'But her heart's still beating.'

I was touched to see that he then stroked her hair affectionately.
They were just a year or two older than me
So I hadn't, in the old days, known them that well.
But I used to be in the circle giving them a yell.

We talked for a while about the bands we had seen
At the 'Fish', Barnet and Cook's Ferry Inn.
And when I told him I'd been too young for the club run by Cy Laurie
He looked at me as if he were genuinely sorry.

Then Madge again murmured: 'Hey diddle, diddle.'
And he retorted: 'Yes, the governor's on the fiddle!'
At which she laughed like a drain and clapped her hands.
'It's the way I tell 'em,' he said with a withering glance

To me. 'Totally lost it—haven't you dear?'
'Hey, diddle, diddle,' she sighed, seeming not to hear.
'But,' he said looking at me, 'just sometimes, funnily enough
When I put on some of the good old stuff

She tries to climb out of her chair for a dance.
 And Humph's "Bad Penny" puts her in a trance.
I keep having to help her up off the carpet
When she hears the left hand of Johnny Parker.

Game old girl, aren't you, dear,'
He said to her fondly. But she seemed not to hear.
'Oh, well,' he sighed fatalistically.
'We got Meals On Wheels coming round at three.

She loves their roast beef and Yorkshire pud.
It really seems to do her good.'
So: "Ooya, ooya!"' he said, giving my shoulder a pat.
'Yes,' I said warmly. 'I'll drink to that!'

Then I watched him trudge away with his cart
And suddenly got a bit of a start
To see him eagerly take from his gear
A large pair of headphones to put on his ears.

And, flicking a switch on some sort of appliance,
As he pushed forward he started to dance.
Jumping two inches up in the air.
As he drummed with his fingers on poor Madge's chair.

'Wuff, wuff,' said Charlie, with a look in his eyes
That suddenly made me realise
Why he'd insisted on bringing me here.
His motive now was abundantly clear:

From my jigging performance the previous night
He thought that I just possibly might
Like to meet a kindred spirit he'd found.
This caring, loving, intelligent hound.

'You're a good old boy, aren't you, Chazz?' said I
And: 'Woof, woof, woof!' was his reply.

*

Soon, throwing sticks and running around
Had worn me out. I needed to sit down.
A wooden bench beneath some trees
Seemed opportune and so I eased
Myself onto the welcome seat
To support my back and rest my feet.

Charlie seemed a bit concerned
He trotted over to check what was wrong.
'Alright, Chazz, I'm just a bit pooped,'
I reassured him as I scooped
Another dead branch from a tree to toss.
'Woof, woof!' he barked then off he was.

Like a bucking bronco trying to get free.
Back legs kicking alarmingly.
He seemed quite happy to play without me
So I leaned back in the bench quite contentedly.
Listening to the birdsong from the trees above:
A lark maybe or a wandering dove.

Could even have been a misplaced pheasant.
But whatever it was it was 'more than pleasant'
So I sat and gazed at the falling dead leaves
Fluttering round in the gentle breeze.
To create a blanket of gold on the ground
Which calmed me with its rustling sound.

But suddenly I got a fright:
That wretched dog was not in sight.
I pushed to my feet in a slight alarm
Hoping it hadn't come to harm.
Or, mild panic crossed my mind,
He'd tried to escape and left me behind.

But I was worrying needlessly
Because I saw Charlie galloping t'wards me
Approaching at enormous speed
Like a stallion in a wild stampede.
The turf vibrated 'neath my feet
From his pounding hooves' quite urgent beat.

It didn't take me very long
To realise there was something wrong.
When Charlie reached me he pawed my chest
Then, barking, did his very best
To tell me what the problem was: 'Woof, woof!'
He said, excitedly. Poking at me with one hoof.

He seemed to be pointing back towards
The part of the park we were in before.
'What is it, Chazz?' I leaned in close
So my left ear rubbed against his nose.
"'A little boy……?" He's "fallen down a well …..?"'
'No!' Chazz pointed again, desperate to tell.

'He's kicked his football into the pond'?
'Wruff, wruff, wruff!' Chazz nodded and….
'Wruff, wruff,.' 'What's that you say?
"Kneeling with a stick?" Well, let's get there right away!'
And without more ado Chazz galloped ahead
While I followed on towards where he led.

I found I was back at that 'bog' again
With water so foul it seemed to come from a drain.
And kneeling there at the edge I saw
A brave little boy of no more than four.
He was stretching out with a stick in his hand
Trying to get a red ball back onto land.

The stick was just a bit short of the ball
And the boy was stretching as if he might fall.
Before I had a chance to really step in
Chazz leapt into the mire and his huge chin
Nudged the ball sideways then pushed it some more
While I held the little boy safe by the shore.

Chazz was a hero but was struggling still
And the boy struggled, too, as most children will.
Then from out of the bushes growing nearby
There strode a blustering, burly, angry big guy.
From his tattooed neck and his aggressive stance
I knew at the first, preliminary glance,

Don't ask me how but I felt I could tell,
The prevailing encounter would not go that well:
'Oi!' The man shouted, coming at me. 'Wha's your 'kin game, pal?'
And, releasing the child, I tried to stand tall.
'Get your slimy 'ands offa my boy!' Something in the gentleman's tone
Made me think he was about to 'stick one on'!

'Now, hang on a minute, mate,' I said indignantly
Just look in the pond and I think that you'll see.
My brave dog and me. We! Have stepped into the breach
When your boy's ball was beyond his reach.'
'Eh?' the man grunted but then he caught the first sight
Of Charlie wet and growling 'Grrrrrrrrrrrr!' and he seemed to take a fright.

'That dog needs a muzzle,' he said, stepping back
As if he felt the beast was going to attack.
'Gurrr!' Chazz was still protesting until I
Patted his wet shoulders saying: 'My,
You're a hero, Chazz, aren't you? But quiet now.
This gentleman just didn't realise how

Good you'd been to help his little boy.
Jumping in that quagmire's not something to enjoy.'
'Yeah, state that water's in's disgusting,' 'Pal' said in a quieter tone.
Then looked at me appeasingly saying: 'Seems like I owe you one.

You and that bruiser dog done great!
And I really do appreciate
That you both had your eyes on my kid.
Wayne!' he called, 'fank this pair f'what they did.'

'And this dog's really got your back, ain't ee?
Don't take no nonsense from no one, do ee!'
'Yeah,' I agreed in colloquial tone
'He's a good old mate. I'm not out alone.'

'You from round 'ere, then?' 'Pal' asked chummily.
'Just over the back,' I told him vaguely.
'What? Those old, Victorian places off the square?'
'Well, yes,' I replied. 'You know it round there?'

'Done a lotta work on them and, gotta say
They don't build their like anymore t'day.'
'Yeah,' I agreed. 'Builders then were craftsmen. No doubt!'
'Well, there are still a few of us about.'

The tattoos on 'Pal's' neck changed shape as he turned his head
To survey the streets beyond the trees, then said:
'And you've got a lovely garden, too I s'pose?'
'Yeah. But neglected a bit. Nothing grows!'

The builder leaned closer and whispered: 'I
Could do you a lovely patio, pal.
And, of course we could arrange, you and me
That there wouldn't be nuffink like Vee A Tee!

Or, a noo baffroom, p'raps,' he said and I tried hard
Not to laugh as he pulled from his pocket a blue business card.
It seemed our relationship had changed just a bit.
I was no longer frightened that I might get hit.
Then, with a handshake that left my hand numb,
He was on his way with his precious young son.

And I glanced at his card and, smiling, thought: I
Might even be tempted to give 'Pal' a try.

'So, Chazz,' I said stroking him with a friendly slap.
'No need for an adult dating app
Or Yellow Pages or such from now, that's agreed.
You can find every service I need.'

And the still soaking dog looked up at me
Saying: 'Wuff, wuff, wuff,' contentedly.

*

I had thoroughly enjoyed our stroll in the park
And Charlie had, too, with barely a bark.
Just a warning growl or two when
He thought I was being threatened; but then,
I'd been grateful for his intervention.
I knew he'd growled with good intention.
So, safely home, I fed him some quorn
Then slumped on the sofa, tired and worn.

Of course, something I'd completely forgotten
Was that the sofa was now the dog's begotten
'Beddy baws' and I found him nudging me with his paws.
Then trying to climb up on all fours.

So I shifted over to make some space
And, climbing up, he licked my face.
A gesture that I didn't quite appreciate
But I knew he was saying: 'I'm your mate!'

Or 'pal' perhaps. So I stroked his back contentedly
And he gave his tail a wag for me.
Yes, Chazz and I were doing alright.
I was a bit ashamed that I'd taken such fright

When Mart had asked me for a favour.
I found that I had been won over.
Our walk in the park had given me
A glimpse of disparate humanity.

People I didn't seem to meet a lot these days.
People like old school 'diamond geezers'
Who, 'between you and me'
Would charge for a job without VAT!

Lonely housewives keen to make a friend
With dogs at their sides to help t'wards that end.
And, best of all, a member of the next generation,
Hoping to preserve for us the thoughts of civilisation.

Thinking these 'Thoughts' led to what I do best:
I fell asleep. (With Charlie's head on my chest.)

*

That evening, Chazz was delighted to find
Strictly Come Dancing on TeeVee. That kind
Of colourful prancing seemed to be
Exactly his preferred cup of tea.

He nodded in time and wuffed a lot
As celebrity guests did a foxtrot
And then growled as one judge for his score
Gave the dancers no more than four.

'Wrrrrruff!' he protested, looking at me.
With a glare so angry that I had to agree.
But then for us both it was early to bed.
No headphones tonight, fitted over my head.

*

I woke up next morning at a quite early hour.
And before checking the dog took a long, hot shower.
I found myself really looking forward to
Getting back to the park to throw a stick or two.

And, downstairs, Charlie, too, seemed keen to get us out there
To the places where we'd been to get his huge great snout there.
Okay, Chazz but some breakfast first
And I need some coffee to quench my thirst.

But, as coffee was brewing, my phone gave me a start
I picked it up and swiped it to hear the voice of Mart.

'Hello, mate. Everything okay?
Your dad's coming home this morning, you say?'
I was really surprised to feel a surge
Of disappointment as I urged

Mart not to hurry back. To take a break
And stay a while: 'I can take
Good care of the dog. We're getting on fine.
He's really become a good, old pal o' mine!'

And I meant exactly what I said.
I looked at Chazz, who nodded his head.
But Mart insisted. Then Jan came on:
'Can you put Charlie on the phone?'

And Chazz seemed to understand
As I held the mobile in my hand.
'Wuff, wuff,' he murmured quietly and
I could hear Jan 'mwuhing' at the other end.

As for me I was almost crying.
And that's the truth! I'm not just lying.
It was hard to contemplate:
I was going to lose my buddy, my newfound mate.

When Jan had finished 'Oochie cooing'.
I took back the phone to ask what they were doing.
'So, when will you get here, mate?' I enquired.
'Ooh! Late afternoon. And we'll be well tired.

Gotta bring dad home. Then pack before we hit the track.'
'There'll be time for "walkies", then, before you get back?'
'If you can be bothered, yeah but no sweat.
You must be sick of Charlie now, I bet.'

Mart couldn't see that my eyes were watering
And I hoped he couldn't hear my voice faltering.
As I looked at the dog and whispered huskily.
'No. Charlie's been really good company.'

Almost as soon as Mart had hung up
I bent down to cuddle the overgrown pup.
'So, mwuh, mwuh, this is "goodbye", Chazz,' I told him and
He gave some soft 'woofs' as he licked my hand.

    *

It seemed to me that Charlie could sense,
Before our 'walkies' even commenced,
That this would be our final outing.
And, on the street, on our way to the park
He gave no soft and gentle bark:
No 'woof', no 'wuff' and a sadness about him
Suggested to me that he, like I,
Was sorry that we were saying goodbye.

But sight of the wrought iron gates of the park
Brought out a gentle bark:
A 'wuff' of glad anticipation
And I could feel the same sensation

As early autumn's soft warm tones
Embraced us on this Sunday morn:
The reds and golds of fallen leaves
Whose moist aroma filled the breeze.

And the paths and grassland were already teeming
With citizens taking the air and beaming.
Laughing couples throwing frisbees.
Others simply walking closely.

Families with children running around
While parents spread large blankets on the ground.
Hindus, Muslims, lapsed Christians, too.
All here to do what people do

On a Sunday morning in the park.
All races gathered, light or dark.
The World was here, unregulated;
British citizens, unsegregated.

Kids of all colours proudly kitted
In the strips of Arsenal or Manchester City.
Long term immigrants or refugees.
Nigerian businessmen and Japanese.

I saw in the distance my mate 'pal'
Out with young Wayne kicking a ball
With two other young kids joining in,
One Chinese, one Indian.

And, as I strolled along with Chazz
A teenage footballer missed a pass
And the ball came bouncing towards me
So I gave it a toe punt, inexpertly.

Towards a fit young Senegalese, or p'raps Samoan
Who called: 'Thanks, mate,' before taking a throw in
To a blonde guy whose ancestors might have landed at Lindisfarne
With a bunch of marauders, heavily armed.

Those Danish pirates: the Viking invaders
Come to plunder, pillage and raid us.
Who knows? Who cares? All that matters is, he's here,
And the Danes do make a lovely beer!

Yes, since the days when Roman Caesars
Venied, Vidied and Vicied to enslave and seize us,
We've had a lot of invading marauders
And, retrospectively, it wasn't that bad for us.

They mostly left us with innovations
That helped this slightly backward nation's
Onward march to future glory.
It's all a part of Mankind's story.

And since the day in ten sixty-six
When William achieved his great Conquest
We haven't been marauded much,
Though from time to time some have tried their luck.

No, in recent centuries
Our visitors have come only in peace
Bearing gifts (mostly of food),
Which have really done the nation good.

Lamb pasanda and chicken peri peri
Which have gone down very, very
Well. Almost replacing our favourite dish
Of greasy chips and battered fish.

While Charlie ran around nearby
I sat on a bench with a happy sigh
To watch the British out at play
On this lovely, sunny autumn day.

There really is no better place
To see first hand the changing face
Of our ancient, noble 'Island Race'
Than the local park on a Sunday morn
Where one can witness the brave, new dawn
Of a Nation being reborn.

With all the old values still intact.
The customs and the dialects.
The well-honed form of colloquial speech.
Still heard in every park or beach.

I found Chazz coming back to play.
And, as I stroked him, I had to say:
'Turned out nice again, hasn't it, eh?'

'Wuff, wuff.'

*

Yvonne was back from Dublin town next day.
And I met her at the airport: 'Hope you enjoyed your stay,'
I said as she kissed me saying: 'It was okay.
But what about you. How'd you get on with the dog, by the way?'

I'd told her several times already on the phone
About the unexpected guest who'd joined me in our home.
'Chazz was good as gold,' I said. 'Liked all your favourite programmes on teevee
And his walkies in the park were really good for me.'

And once we were in a taxi I opened up some more:
'I've been thinking about the patio, love. I'm sure
That we could improve the layout: new tiles on the ground.
I want to try a local builder that I've found.

Oh, and by the way. I've cancelled my subscription to that adult dating site.
I've got to say: it wasn't worth a light.
When Charlie took me walkies I found a better plan:
The park is full of single women looking for a man.

All after a night of "hot, raw sex"!
No need to even send a text.'
'Well, I have to say, my pet.
They might be disappointed with what they get!'

'Ohhhh! Woof, woof. Grrrrrr. Come over here
And let me bite your blinking ear!'

* * *

This piece really has no place in the current collection. It came to me in the summer of 1979 as a madrigal, woven loosely around Charlie Parker's 'Parker's Mood', when I was struggling uphill to one of Lisbon's Belvederes.

I turned around suddenly and was startled to find the whole of Lisbon spread beneath me and a voice in my head said: 'Bid this world you have known: "Goodbye!"' By the time I reached the top of the hill and sat on a wall to get my breath back, I realised the voice was talking not to me but to that star-crossed lover, Romeo Montagu.

I worked on the piece in my head for a year and had the main lyric more or less intact but could not come up with satisfactory lines for the slightly plainsong chant that underpins the piece. I then took a copy of Mr Shakespeare's play to the isle of Rhodes when I was on holiday with a girlfriend of the time in 1980 and found, towards the end of the drama, an exclamation of Lady Capulet's that fitted perfectly.

I completed the piece (and its accompanying melody,) when I got home and put it in a cupboard. No one has seen it and, certainly, no choir has ever sung it. So I thought: why not slip it in here? I hope my readers will bear with my self-indulgence.

Juliet Adieu

The world's watching you.
We're all lovers, too ...

Oh, people in the street cry: 'Romeo'.
People in the street cry: 'Romeo'.
But what of love's wild passion do they know?

*

Bid your adored young bride: 'goodbye'.
You will not wake her again.
You only shake her in vain.
For you'll not take her again.
Don't try.

And she was such a young bride to die.
Hardly a child, no more.
Still a mere child before
She was beguiled by your
Deep sigh.

And, lonely, in those musky, dew-soaked mornings
As the dawn you fled,
Was this the dream that filled your young man's head?

Well, see your dream spread
On her cold wedding bed.
Awf'lly and unalterably dead!

*

Oh, people in the street cry: 'Romeo'.

But there is no need that you even should heed them
Pay their distant cries no mind.
You're on your way now to find some kind of freedom.
Leave this bitter world behind.

Your young life is here consigned
Unto Destiny's design.

*

You were the jewel of all Verona.
A nobleman's sole son and heir.
You'd've had maidens to spare.
Just waved your hand in the air.
But: no!

Juliet, too, aroused all who'd known her.
She could have lingered a while.
Led them all on with a smile.
She'd've been courted in style.
But: no!

Were there ever two such uncorrupted children?
Pure as fresh fallen snow.
Oh but, Juliet, wherefore Romeo?

For didn't you know
Your fam'ly were foe?
And so did love like some dread cancer grow.

*

Oh, people in the street cry: 'Romeo'!

But you can hold everything there on the brink, now.
Stay the final, chosen pain.
There is no need that you leave this world thinking
That your young life was all in vain.

Romeo,
Don't you know?

You've lived far more than many men
Who've seen their threescore years and ten

For you rose up and took a command of
The traffic on your tiny stage.
And in one brief burst of bold manhood
Boy, you surely came of age.

Romeo,
I swear it's so.
What use clinging to your mortal soul
Once old age has turned your lifeblood cold?

Look hard on the town's noble 'made men'
Grown coarse and gross with wealth.
Or see yesterday's lovely young maidens
Turned harridans by Time's cruel stealth.

Romeo,
You must know:
It was never that dark demon Death
That sucked the honey from their virgin breath.

Oh, people in the street cry: 'Romeo'!
But what of love's young passion do they know?

*

Here in the dark as you view Death's portal,
All sense of grief is misplaced

No need to weep your life's waste,
For you're not dying disgraced.
Not you.

Love's wild spark has made you immortal.
And generations to come
Will venerate what you've done.
Nobles will name their first son
For you.

So don't think yourself the poor blind fool to fortune.
That was never true.
Just go ahead and do what you must do.

The world's watching you.
We're all lovers, too.
So bid your darling Juliet:
'Adieu!'

* * *